READY TO QUIT YOUR JOB?

Copyright © Yeşim Nicholson 2024

ISBN 9798884729582

First published March 2024

The right of Yeşim Nicholson to be identified as author of this work has been asserted by her in accordance with the Copyright, Designs and Patents Act 1988.

The print publication is protected by copyright. Prior to any prohibited reproduction, storage in a retrieval system, distribution or transmission in any form or by any means, electronic, mechanical, recording or otherwise, permission should be obtained from the author or, where applicable, a licence permitting restricted copying in the United Kingdom should be obtained from Yeşim Nicholson.

The ePublication is protected by copyright and must not be copied, reproduced, transferred, distributed, leased, licensed or publicly performed or used in any way except as specifically permitted in writing by the author, as allowed under the terms and conditions under which it was purchased, or as strictly permitted by applicable copyright law. Any unauthorised distribution or use of this text may be a direct infringement of the author's rights and those responsible may be liable in law accordingly.

All trademarks used herein are the property of their respective owners. The use of any trademark in this text does not vest in the author any trademark ownership rights in such trademarks, nor does the use of such trademarks imply any affiliation with or endorsement of this book by such owners.

Yeşim Nicholson is not responsible for the content of third-party internet sites.

READY TO QUIT YOUR JOB?

Your guide to a much more fulfilling career

FIRST EDITION

Yeşim Nicholson

Contents

PART 1 – GETTING STARTED — 1
   Who is this book for? — 2
   How to get the most out of this book — 5
   About me — 7
   Oh crystal ball, tell me all! — 10

PART 2 – WHERE ARE YOU NOW? — 19
   Why you're feeling disgruntled in your current work — 20
   How did you end up here? — 22
   What's motivating you? — 29
   'Moving away from' motivations — 30
   'Moving towards' motivations — 35
   Seeking equilibrium — 41
   Why you haven't quit yet — 43
   Your identity – Who are you anyway? — 68
   You think you're too old — 71
   You don't know what to do — 74

PART 3 – (RE)DISCOVERING YOU — 75
   Finding the joy — 76
   Remember who you are? — 79
   Your unique blend — 83
   Your superpowers — 86
   You just haven't experienced it yet — 89

PART 4 – DESIGN — 93
   Defining success — 95
   Career mission statement — 98
   Your job description — 100
   The right environment — 105
   Stop spending time on job search platforms... for now — 107
   Refuse to choose: Becoming a multi-hyphenate — 108

PART 5 – IT'S ALL IN YOUR MIND   111
    Regret-proofing   113
    Step out of your comfort zone   114
    The luck factor   117
    What are you paying attention to?   121
    What's coming out of your mouth?   123
    Mindfulness   127
    Meditation   129
    Mindful activities   133
    Manifestation   135
    Creating a vision board   136
    Confidence   139
    Curiosity killed the cat   144

PART 6 – YOUR BODY   145
    Forming new habits   146
    Your health   150
    The power of sleep   154
    Nutrition   156

PART 7 – EXPLORING WHAT'S POSSIBLE   159
    A change of scenery   160
    Taking time out   162
    Skill up   166
    Be, Do, Have... Give   167
    Starting a side hustle   171
    Volunteering   175
    Find a stopgap   176
    Working part-time   177
    Seek out a secondment   181
    Research   182

PART 8 – YOUR PEOPLE   183
    Your support network   185
    Cheerleaders   186
    Coach   187
    Role models   188
    Dealing with people who don't want you to make a change   189

PART 9 – CONCLUSION — 197

What's it going to be? — 198
Handing in your resignation — 200
The U-turn — 201
Short-term pain, long-term gain — 202
Patience and faith — 203
Plan B — 204
One final thing — 205
Thank yous — 207

PART 1
Getting started

Who is this book for?

*"Should I stay or should I go now?
If I go, there will be trouble
And if I stay it will be double"*

THE CLASH

Indecision is mind-numbing and a real energy-sapper. It's a breeding ground for self-doubt and inactivity. Endlessly going round in circles and not knowing which way to turn makes us feel stuck. Big life decisions are rarely made easily, and on a whim.

There's so much to consider, so much at stake. The mere thought of stepping into the unknown comes with inevitable dread that things might not turn out how you'd like them to. Your decision is likely to affect your income, your standard of living and your relationship with family and friends in ways that even the most skilled clairvoyant couldn't predict.

If you've been thinking about jumping ship for days, weeks, months or even years, and you feel like you're at a crossroads, then this book is for you. It will provide a guiding light, making the decision as stress free as possible, and maybe even enjoyable.

This book is not an opinion piece on whether you should quit your job or not. My opinion, quite frankly, doesn't matter. In fact I don't really have an opinion on whether you should quit or not. I do however feel strongly about the fact that if you're unhappy in your current position, you should 100 per cent do something about it.

Whether they're conscious of it or not, most people seek meaning, control and fun in their work.

Why? Because when your job aligns with your passions, values and interests, something magical happens. Your job becomes more than a means to earn a living; it becomes a constant source of inspiration, purpose, positive energy and joy. Please show me someone who doesn't want that in their life?

Have you ever noticed how people who love their work tend to have a vitality about them – a spring in their step? They're more playful, and often have a sparkle in their eyes. I wish this for you. I wish this for everyone because I genuinely believe in the positive effect our happiness (and therefore our words and actions) can have on those around us. I hope, like the people you'll read about in this book, you find true contentment and joy in your work again.

If you have dreams of doing something extraordinary, of following your passion, of fulfilling your deepest desires, then perhaps now is your time to shine. Take some kind of step towards fulfilling your ambitions, even if it's just a baby step. Do it now. Life is short. Life is precious. It's time to start treating it as such.

> *"The wealthiest place on the planet is the graveyard, because in the graveyard we will find inventions that we were never ever exposed to, ideas, dreams that never became a reality, hopes and aspirations that were never acted upon."*
>
> LES BROWN

In this book, I'll share with you facts based on evidence, plenty of research and real-life examples to help answer some of your questions and eliminate doubts that have held you back from making a decision and – perhaps more importantly – taking action.

While there are many reasons to feel excited about changing your career path, the reality is that it is often an intense and challenging journey. A journey that is worth being very well prepared for. When you go on holiday, or a journey of any kind, there are things that need to be thought through and planned. Where are you going, who are you going with, how will you get there, how much will it cost, what do we need to pack, how will you finance it, do you have insurance?

Considering the average person will spend 90,000 hours of their life working, it's worth getting right, don't you agree?

If you read every page of this book, you'll be safe in the knowledge that quitting your job hasn't been a knee-jerk reaction. Rather it has been a carefully thought-out decision to get you closer to a career – and life – that you'll love.

How to get the most out of this book

The aim of this book is to challenge you and your belief systems, to open your eyes to possibilities, to give you practical advice on how to decide whether you should quit your job (or not), and what to do next.

It is designed for you to indulge in some truly insightful self-reflection and exploration. It will require a level of vulnerability. The purpose is to get you to think and act differently.

Be prepared for a profound shift.

> *"The definition of insanity is doing the same thing over and over and expecting different results."*
>
> ALBERT EINSTEIN

Be open, trust the process and, for goodness sake, please have some fun with it. Us adults do have a nasty habit of taking ourselves far too seriously. In the words of the wise Oscar Wilde "life is too important to be taken seriously". Yes, your career is important, but this doesn't mean you can't have some fun exploring a career that makes you happy.

There are many questions and exercises throughout the book that will challenge and provoke you so I recommend that you always have a notebook and pen handy.

Did you know research has shown that handwriting can do some pretty cool things to our brain? For a start, it forces us to slow down. And for those of us who frequently use keyboards or phones, it encourages our brains to work in a different way – unleashing creativity and increasing neural activity in sections of the brain, creating optimal conditions for learning.

Apart from posing questions to get you to think differently and hopefully giving you a few 'aha' moments, I'll be sharing real stories of people who have made changes in their careers. Some anecdotes are excerpts from people who were kind enough to share their stories on my podcast 'Your Big Career Move'. Some are from clients I've worked with. Some are from conversations I struck up with virtual strangers. May their stories inspire and delight you!

About me

It's unlikely that you've picked up this book to read all about me. So if you want to skip this bit and get to the juicy bits that are all about YOU, I won't be in the slightest bit offended.

Here's a little insight into how I've ended up working with people who want to make a career change, and writing a book to help you decide whether or not you're ready to quit *your* job.

Five years into my first job post-university, I wanted to quit. My reasons for wanting to leave were very clear, but fear had been holding me back from taking the leap into the unknown.

When I wrote a list of reasons why I was scared to leave and read them back to myself, I suddenly realised just how insignificant they were when compared with my biggest fear. A fear which had played on repeat in my mind during my early 20s.

I had a vision of sitting next to someone very interesting at a dinner party – aged in my 80s – and saying I had worked a corporate gig at Motorola all my life. What I wanted to be able to say was that I'd experienced everything life had to offer – and that it'd been one heck of a journey!

That's what ultimately gave me the fire in my belly to hand in my resignation with very sweaty palms.

I was young. I had no real ties or responsibilities, but I did feel I needed my parents' approval – they had funded my education after all. I fully expected them to convince me to stay in my stable, well-paid job (that was boring me to tears). Receiving their blessing was a kind of litmus test. Luckily, they had recently embarked on their own entrepreneurial journey, and I think they therefore recognised the fire in my belly.

And so began a journey that has taken me around the world and built me into the person I am today.

Some of the many jobs I've had over the years include:

- Project manager for the creation of an agriculture university in Uzbekistan.
- After-sales support in Germany.
- Founder of an e-commerce business.
- Founder of a marketing consultancy.
- Business adviser in the UK.
- Kids' entertainer at a hotel in Turkey.
- Receptionist at an acupuncture clinic in Australia.

Did I love each one of the many roles I took on over the years? No!

Was it easy making the transition in between each role? Definitely not!

Did they each teach me something and guide me towards the things I love today? Absolutely!

Did I learn more about myself and my natural strengths through these experiences than the majority of my peers who stuck to their predictable corporate roles? Without a shadow of a doubt.

But I credit my somewhat nomadic upbringing (my dad was a hotel manager) with my biggest gift – the ease and speed with which I can adapt and thrive in new situations.

Which is why I love that I now get to help people from all walks of life – in any and every career you could imagine – to overcome their fears, and find the inner confidence and courage to make positive changes to their lives.

I hope you enjoy my first book!

Oh crystal ball, tell me all!

So why have you *really* picked up this book? Perhaps you're looking for 'permission' to quit your job. Maybe you're feeling lost and aren't able to talk to your nearest and dearest about how discontented you're feeling. It's possible that you *have* spoken to them, but they're not willing or able to support you in the way you need to be supported right now. Whatever your reason, from the bottom of my heart, I hope you find courage and inspiration on these pages. If you're feeling lost, I hope you find yourself again.

When I started working with people who wanted to make a career change, I held a perhaps slightly naive assumption that everyone I worked with would indeed end up changing their career path. I was wrong! It very quickly became apparent that by the time they finished working with me, everyone fell into one of four categories. I can guarantee that by reading this book you will too. Which one will it be?

Remainer
Tweaker
Toe dipper
Leaper ™

If, in the six months after reading this book, you don't fall into one of these categories, I'd love to hear from you.

Let me explain what each category means.

Remainer

Having read, carefully considered and explored your options, you may find that your attitude to your existing work has changed and you've discovered a new zest for it. You may realise that all you needed to feel good about your career again was a shift in mindset. You may find that reading this book gives you a confidence boost and encourages you to show up in a more positive, energised way – where you feel less stuck and have a newfound appreciation and gratitude for your work. This won't go unnoticed by your colleagues, your boss and possibly even your family and friends.

This can happen for a number of reasons. Sometimes when you take time out to really appreciate what you've achieved you realise that you have indeed got a lot to be proud of. If your younger self could see you now, there's a good chance they'd be impressed.

There is a danger of blaming work for our general discontentment. Adopting an overall more positive mindset, which I hope this book will do for you, will often lead to a fresh, more uplifting attitude to work and life on the whole.

I've worked with countless professionals who felt they needed a complete career change because they were so unhappy in their jobs. However, after working together for just a few weeks, something extraordinary and quite wonderful happened: they started to remember things about themselves they'd forgotten. They unearthed skills they hadn't been using; interests and passions they'd somehow forgotten along the way.

They stopped focusing their attention on the annoying colleague who undermined them. The commute that they dreaded turned into an opportunity to learn about a new hobby or interest they'd discovered through meaningful self-reflection.

It's easy to get caught up in the day-to-day, and focus on getting through the multitude of tasks that land in our inbox. When we don't take time out we can lose sight of how we're actually spending our days.

Change for change's sake

I've worked with people who have been in the same, or similar, job for several years and think they *have* to make a change. They see others following their dreams and feel a degree of envy because they are unable to follow suit for whatever reason. Other times it's because they see people around them being promoted, and this makes them feel like their career has plateaued, that they're somehow being left behind.

Don't fall into the trap of making a change for change's sake. Just because you have a niggly feeling that you *should* be doing something else, doesn't always mean it's right for you.

> *"The foolish man* seeks happiness in the distance; the wise grows it under his feet."*
>
> JAMES OPPENHEIM

(*presumably this applies to women too, but James lived in a time when women mattered less)

Meet Tracey

Tracey was at a point in her career where she felt restless and unfulfilled. By the end of my group career change programme, she was showing up to work a much more confident person. She started putting herself forward to get involved in projects she previously wouldn't have had the self-belief or headspace to do. What's more, her new attitude didn't go unnoticed; people started to approach her to be part of new and exciting projects, which were far more aligned with her strengths and interests. When we caught up a few weeks later, she beamed: "I'm one million per cent a better me".

Maybe Tracey will make a big career change at some point, but at the time of writing, she's simply much more content in her current work.

Tweaker

Maybe you'll end up being a Tweaker as a result of reading this book. Just like the Remainer, you may come to the conclusion that staying where you are is in fact going to be a viable option for you for the foreseeable future.

Unlike the Remainer however, you create an action plan for yourself which focuses on making tweaks to your current work. This could be working from home more, or less. It could be asking to take on more, or less, responsibility. You might finally pluck up the courage to ask for the pay rise you feel you deserve. You may put yourself forward and get involved in new projects. Asking to join the 'fun' team in your organisation is also an option.

A Tweaker is on the hunt and actively looking for opportunities within their existing work to make it more fun, more fulfilling, more challenging, less stressful, and more in line with their strengths, values and needs.

Meet Elizabeth

Elizabeth thrives on new challenges and has steadily worked her way up the career ladder over the past 20 years. She's great at what she does, is comfortably rewarded and finds joy in her work and the people she works with. Yet for a while there had been a niggly voice in her head that made her wish she was using some of her untapped skills. Elizabeth had always enjoyed performing and very much identified as a 'people person'. So when her company was looking for someone to co-host its new podcast, she put herself forward. She is now the co-host of an award-winning podcast, and it's one of the highlights of her career – despite the fact that 'podcast host' was never part of her original job description.

Elizabeth is the perfect example of someone who has tweaked their existing job to make it more fun, fulfilling and meaningful. By finding an opportunity to get involved with a project that is outside of her immediate responsibility she has gained a whole new zest for life.

What 'fun' opportunities are on offer at your current organisation? What could you put yourself forward for that requires a skill you'd love to use and showcase?

Meet Sean

During the Covid lockdown, like so many of us, Sean started working from home. When restrictions were lifted his organisation offered all employees the opportunity to 'work from anywhere'. As the office was a two-hour commute, he made the decision to find a local co-working space to work from. After a year of working remotely, he became very conscious of the fact that he was less engaged and enjoying his work less than he used to. It wasn't until he was asked to attend a meeting at the office that he realised that what he'd been missing was the feeling of being part of something exciting. "I just got a real buzz from being around my team again. It was like I received an injection of motivation, and now I've fallen back in love with my job".

Sean made a small tweak, and now visits his London headquarters every fortnight.

Toe-dipper

Things are hotting up now. While the Remainer and the Tweaker have a little bit of work to do, the Toe-dipper has a bigger challenge on their hands. Love a challenge? Read on.

You may, having carefully considered everything in this book, decide that you will stay in your current role for the time being, but put some serious work into exploring your new career, with the view of quitting your job in the not-so-distant future. You might do this in the form of a side hustle, which is a small business you get up and running in your spare time – for most people, this is evenings and weekends. You may use any spare time to explore other career opportunities by volunteering or taking on a part-time role.

Being a Toe-dipper gives you the perfect opportunity to work on passion projects. Start with an interest that you have, spend time exploring it, and see where it leads you.

Meet Hannah

Like so many others, Hannah worried that her career as a commercial airline pilot might come to a permanent end when all flights were grounded in the UK during Covid lockdowns. Not one to sit around awaiting her fate, she took matters into her own hands. She'd always had a keen interest in health and wellbeing, and decided to qualify as a sports massage therapist. She converted the spare room in her home into a treatment room, and when restrictions were lifted she started to treat her first clients. When she was called to fly again, she continued her massage therapy business around her rota, thereby combining her love of flying with her love of health and wellbeing.

Leaper

As the name suggests, you may read this book and decide that right now is absolutely the right time for you to take the leap, quit your job and do that thing that will bring you joy and a sense of purpose. You've done your research, you've worked out your finances, you've worked through the things that are holding you back, and you take the big leap of faith towards your new future.

With fire in your belly and a robust plan, you're ready to take on your new world. There are exciting times ahead for you, that will no doubt challenge and reward you. It's time to say goodbye to a job that's been serving you – perhaps in more ways than one – but that you know deep down won't be right for you in the future. The time has come for you to spend your precious days on work that makes you want to jump out of bed every morning and thank the heavens that you get to spend yet another glorious day doing what you love.

No one outcome is better or worse than the other. No one is here to cast judgement on what you ultimately decide. It's *your* life. It's *your* journey. Whichever category you end up falling into is fine. Actually it's more than fine. If you've given yourself the gift of taking the time and effort to explore your career options, you are 100 steps ahead of most people. Why? Because most people stumble through life never taking time to reflect on their contribution to the world. They never wonder whether they could be happier, more productive, wealthier, more successful.

You are extraordinary!

As someone very wise once said, "The only constant thing is change." Just because you don't make a massive career change as soon as you've read the final page of this book doesn't mean that you haven't made major progress and taken important steps towards feeling happier in your work.

Why not take a moment to reflect right now and write down which of the four outcomes feels like it's the most likely for you at this point? Will you be a Remainer, Tweaker, Toe-dipper or Leaper™?

I'll ask you again at the end. I'm curious to know whether you were right.

PART 2
Where are you now?

Why you're feeling disgruntled in your current work

How clear are you on the reasons you're considering quitting your job? If you're feeling disgruntled, but you haven't taken the time to properly analyse where the dissatisfaction is stemming from, it's a good idea to become crystal clear about your reasons. It's not uncommon to blame work for our unhappiness when sometimes it's far from the root cause. Often, it's merely a convenient scapegoat.

Here are some signs that you may be in the wrong job; perhaps some of these will strike a chord with you:

- You're bored and not being challenged in the right way.
- You're not using (m)any of your skills and strengths.
- Your job involves too many activities which drain you of energy, and not enough that energise you.
- You feel like you're surrounded by all the wrong people.
- You're working for the wrong organisation.
- You're not receiving any recognition or appreciation for your brilliant work.
- You find it hard to get out of bed in the morning.
- You're grumpy at the end of each working day, but actually quite jolly at weekends (or other non-working days).
- You're not sleeping well.
- You're constantly worrying about work.

- You feel like you're working 'hard' but don't experience any sense of satisfaction.
- If you were to win enough money in the lottery tomorrow, you'd quit your job before your winnings have even hit your bank account.
- Your health is suffering – you get constant headaches, you have strange rashes, you're gaining too much weight.

How did you end up here?

There are many reasons people don't enjoy their work, and sometimes those reasons aren't as obvious as we think. If you're in a career or job you don't love anymore, perhaps never have, and are wondering how the heck you've ended up there, you are not alone. I've had the privilege of working with hundreds of people who have reached a point in their life where carrying on with the status quo is no longer an option. Just like you, they want – sometimes desperately *need* – change.

For some reason many of us don't invest the time in ourselves to truly reflect on our career. We get busy with the day-to-day. Running around after kids, housework, pets, social life. All these commitments that you feel forced to focus your attention on. Yet, many of us spend more time mindlessly scrolling on social media and watching endless Netflix box sets than thinking about how our next career move will serve us.

Why? Because the easy option, more often than not, is carrying on with the familiar. Taking the time to think about how our career and life could be better takes time and effort. And often we haven't even spent the time getting clear on what 'better' really means.

Recently I spoke to someone who described himself as shallow because he hadn't taken any time in the last few years to consider what made him happy. He was simply going through the motions; getting through the day; doing what he needed to do to grow his business.

The truth is that this is very normal for a vast majority of people, but the reason we end up in this situation is not because we are shallow. It's often much more complex.

Let's explore some of the reasons you may have drifted off course and are in a job that is no longer aligned with who you are.

They made me do it

Many of us fall into jobs or follow a career path that we believe is expected of us. You excelled at maths at school so your career adviser suggested becoming an accountant was the obvious choice. Or you come from a family in which generation after generation has followed the same career path; who are you to break the cycle? Perhaps your parents had dreams and aspirations for you that weren't up for discussion. Sometimes our parents are very vocal and clear about what they expect from us. Other times their expectations are expressed more subtly. But they're there nevertheless.

Maybe your spouse insisted on a certain lifestyle, and your current and future potential salary was, to their mind, the only way to fund it.

Basically you were strongly encouraged to follow a certain career path, and never put too much time and thought into whether it was something you actually wanted to do. Or maybe you did, but were coerced into doing it anyway.

I'm so good at it, I couldn't not

There's a misconception that merely being good at something, and being able to do that thing in our work will make for a happy and successful career. Have you fallen victim to the 'curse of the strength'? Have you fallen into the trap of recognising that you have above average capability in an area, and designed your entire career around that? Only to find that doing that thing day in, day out brings you next to no joy at all? I've lost count of the number of people I've spoken to who have followed a certain career path because they showed an aptitude for it.

You may be familiar with the Peter Principle: you do a good job, your organisation wants to reward you, they promote you into a role with more responsibility, but that isn't necessarily suited to you. You start to underperform, get stressed and feel resentful. All because you showed such promise!

It was all an accident

Unless you were lucky enough to have someone in your life who spotted and encouraged your genius when you were little, you may feel like you've ended up where you are by complete fluke.

You never really knew what you wanted to do, so applied for jobs that vaguely interested you after you finished your education, and took the first job you were offered. You've accidentally fallen into your career, and have followed a path that's been a series of 'accidents'.

My own research shows that almost 70 per cent of people end up in their career accidentally, so if your career has developed through a series of unplanned events, you're in good company.

It has served its purpose, now it's time to move on

Has the work you've been doing served its purpose? There's an assumption that just because something has worked for you in the past, it will continue to work for you in the future. This is not necessarily the case. Now it's time to find something that will serve the next chapter of your life.

One of my absolute career highlights was taking on the management of a brand new space to bring together local businesses. The idea was that business owners would be welcomed into a beautiful purpose-built building with a co-working space, specialised one-to-one advice, workshops and events all on offer.

The role ticked all the boxes for me. I got to meet new, interesting people every day. I worked in a stunning environment. I managed a small, yet perfectly formed team of amazing people. I curated events that I thought might interest and benefit local businesses. I played a big part in creating and fostering a supportive community. I was fairly well paid. I worked three days a week. It was fun; it was challenging; it was exciting. No two days were the same.

So I can't blame my father for questioning my decision to leave after four years. He reminded me that a few months into the role, I had told him that this was my dream job and I absolutely loved it. From this statement, it seems, he drew the conclusion that this was a job I would do until the day I died – or retired. He seemed disappointed in my decision to leave. And his disappointment resulted in me really taking the time to question why I felt it was time to move on.

Perhaps this resonates with you. Perhaps someone who is important to you has demonstrated disappointment in your desire to leave your current role and start something new. Perhaps you fear letting them down.

Luckily, I had spent a lot of time over the years reflecting on, and becoming crystal clear about, what makes me tick. I knew myself very well, and I knew that what had been exciting to me about the role was taking a concept and making it a reality. I loved the 'newness' of it. Making sure the building site turned into an inviting, thriving and useful space. Hiring the perfect team. Promoting the space and services we offered to attract just the right customer.

Once the space was up and running just as I'd envisaged, there was very little challenge left for me. The day-to-day operations just didn't energise me. Conversely, my colleagues thrived on ensuring we kept things ticking over, and I was more than happy to hand the reins to them. The role had served its purpose.

You could have had a really great career to date. You can be outrageously proud of what you've achieved. Your work may have given you all you could have ever asked for in terms of prestige, security, remuneration and excitement. If you ultimately decide, having read this book, that it is in fact time for you to move onto something new, don't feel bad about what you may be leaving behind. Be thankful for the opportunity, the experiences, the people and the lessons you learned along the way. You'll take them all with you. They have shaped you into the person you are today and will most probably serve you well in your next chapter.

When I interviewed Sarah for my podcast, she shared an analogy in which she likened her career to a pair of shoes – that had fit her perfectly and were very comfortable for many years. However, when you're getting ready to run a new race, she said, they may not be the right shoe for you anymore. They eventually stop serving their purpose. "It's okay if something that we built and we were proud of and we put all this effort into – if that doesn't serve us anymore. We are not the same people at 40 that we were when we were 20, and we're not the same people at 60 as we were when we were 40."

Your circumstances change. You change. Your priorities change. So doesn't it make sense that what you need and want from your work changes too?

I've had countless conversations with people who don't think that you should question whether or not you could be happier in your work. What frivolity! They think that work is a means to an end. It's a way to keep a roof over their heads. A way to keep themselves and their family fed. Some genuinely work hard, just so they can enjoy their retirement. Unfortunately none of us are guaranteed to reach retirement age. How many people do you know who haven't been lucky enough to live to midlife, never mind retirement age? Life is happening right here, right now. Don't waste it with resentment, frustration, stress, anger and anxiety.

Whether we realise it or not, we're all aiming for happiness and contentment. We just go about it in different, and sometimes completely warped and illogical, ways.

Try this

Take five minutes to write down what factors have led you to the career you have today. Some of the questions you can ask yourself are:

- Is your career to date an amalgamation of a series of deliberate decisions and actions?
- What was the main driver behind the decisions?
- Which people have influenced your career most?
- What are the strengths that you've used along the way?
- What are some of your most joyful, treasured memories when you look back over your career?

In summary, there are lots of reasons we end up in a career that feels like it's been curated for us by an alien.

But can we make a pact, right now, to stop using those reasons as an excuse to not move forward and make changes that are going to make you a much better person to be around?

What's motivating you?

People leave secure jobs every day to pursue their dream career. As you can imagine their motivations to do so vary vastly. What's motivating you to quit your job? What motivated you to even pick up this book?

Looking at it simply, our motivations fall into two categories: we are either moving *towards* something (pleasure) or *away* from something (pain).

Put another way, change is generally sparked by 'inspiration' or 'desperation'. In some cases it's a combination of the two.

You don't feel valued by your organisation (pain) and have a dream of being a motivational speaker (pleasure). You don't get paid enough in your current role to pay your bills (pain) and you love the idea of being a stockbroker (pleasure). In many ways having a bit of each is the perfect combination. You may have a clear idea of what you'd rather be doing, but without experiencing pain points in your current work, it's too easy to stay put and not follow your dream.

Whatever your motivation, it's always sensible to start with an understanding of what is driving you to want to make a change.

I've outlined some of the motivations I've come across over the years. See which one resonates with you. Perhaps it's all of them, or just a handful.

'Moving away from' motivations

Your health is suffering

There are few things that give us a stronger wakeup call than failing health. Heart attacks, depression, anxiety, panic attacks, curious rashes, gastrointestinal problems, extreme weight gain or loss, migraines... the list goes on. Sometimes we don't realise just how stressed and burnt out we are until our health starts to deteriorate.

Our bodies tend to give us little warning signs in the beginning. You may feel more tired than usual, or start comfort eating. If we don't listen to those early, gentle signs, the symptoms get worse, until we finally sit up and take note.

If you have a job that requires you to be 'on' all the time, this may seem fun and exhilarating in the moment, but can have a detrimental effect on our health in the long-term. We're quite able to deal with short bouts of stress, but we are definitely not designed to be in a constant state of fight or flight. So if you're in a job where you're constantly in stress mode and you have little or no time to recover, your body will start to let you know that this is not okay.

Stress can be caused by a multitude of things such as lack of autonomy, too much responsibility, the sheer volume of work or your work not aligning with your values.

Unfortunately I've met far too many people who chose to ignore the warning signs and this ended up severely impacting their short- and sometimes long-term health.

Meet Jen

Jen had a successful career in a big wealth management company. She started experiencing frequent migraines and was constantly feeling exhausted before she hit rock bottom and felt completely stuck. She found an understanding GP, who took the time to look at the cause of her symptoms rather than just offering a pill to mask them. This led to the realisation that she didn't have to keep pretending everything was okay. Being signed off from work for a couple of months for depression gave her time to reflect on her life and what was important to her. Working with a coach helped her to unpick the belief that she was stuck and tap back into her vision of what she actually wanted. She realised her work wasn't feeding her soul and a part of her had been shut away.

> *"I'd built myself a beautiful cage."*

She recalls being judged by her partner (who she's no longer with) and being told that "you can't hug trees for a living". When I interviewed her for my podcast, she took great delight in sharing that you can in fact get paid to do exactly that. Having left her corporate role and retrained as a coach and wild facilitator, she now works with women to help them reconnect with themselves through reconnecting with nature. Her amazing retreats take women into nature, and there is most definitely some tree hugging involved!

You're bored

Another motivating factor for seeking a change is boredom. This is talked about and acknowledged much less frequently, because many don't consider boredom a good enough reason to make change. However, tedium *is* a legitimate reason to pursue new challenges. Spending your days doing tasks that drain you of energy, with little or no stimulation, can have a negative impact on your wellbeing, especially if you have an eagerness to learn and grow as a person.

There's every chance you're not using any of the skills you've developed over the years or the natural talents you were born with. When was the last time you felt a sense of pride or achievement in your work? Is there anything more disheartening than working hard, but ultimately not having a positive association with your work anymore? Put simply, you're bored and have fallen out of love with your current role.

Your relationships are suffering

You may be looking to get out of your current role because you know your job is affecting your relationship with the people who matter to you most. Your partner, your kids, your parents, your friends. You're grumpy and offhand because you're tired at the end of the working day. You're constantly preoccupied and thinking about work, even at weekends and while on holiday.

Are you a good person to be around if you're coming home from a job that's giving you absolutely no joy whatsoever?

You don't feel appreciated in your current role

Is there anything more demoralising than being dedicated to and great at your role, but receiving no recognition for it? Recognition can come in the form of financial compensation. It could be some kind of award. As a bare minimum, it could be genuine appreciation from a boss, colleague, mentor or indeed a customer. Being appreciated for your work is something everyone should experience *at least* once in a lifetime, because it feels so damn good.

The flip side, of course, is never experiencing how it feels to please someone with the work you do. It can make you and the work you do feel unimportant and insignificant. I don't know about you, but I don't know many people who don't want to feel important and significant in some way.

> *"There are no unimportant jobs, just people who feel unimportant in their jobs."*
>
> MARK SANBORN, AUTHOR OF *THE FRED FACTOR*

Your values aren't aligned with your organisation's

When our personal values aren't aligned with those of the organisation we work for, we can experience decreased motivation, self-doubt or a general sense of discontentment. Fundamentally disagreeing with how the people within your organisation – notably senior management – conduct themselves can be extremely confronting. Not being able to influence and challenge how things get done when it goes against your core values can be debilitating.

A client told me, "I found myself justifying and defending my organisation's actions to customers, stakeholders and sometimes even friends and family. I felt that if I didn't, it would reflect badly on me. But over time it wore me down. I didn't believe half the things I was saying anymore. It made me feel sick to my stomach."

If you're the CEO it's more likely you can influence the organisation's core values and culture. If you're lower down the chain, that's a much harder task and a challenge few are willing to take on. Leaving the establishment in search of an employer who shares your values may appear to be your best option.

'Moving towards' motivations

You want to do something more meaningful

I've lost count of the number of people who tell me they just want to do something more meaningful or purposeful. Like so many others, you may have fallen into, and then pursued, a career without giving it too much thought.

When many of us get to a certain point in our life, we start to confront the sometimes-harsh realities of our career aspirations. Something happens that makes us take stock of our lives, and very few of us come to the conclusion that all is hunky dory and can carry on in blissful harmony.

We've been striving to do well in our careers, to provide for our families, to make our parents proud, to impress our peers and to keep up with the Joneses. We're on the hedonic treadmill, and it starts to dawn on us that the treadmill isn't getting us anywhere anymore. How much wealth and material possessions can we accumulate?

The truth is that many of us will bumble through life never really knowing or bothering to ask ourselves what our purpose is.

Others will begin to question what their contribution to the world is and what legacy they want to leave behind.

Some will beat themselves up if they don't know what their true calling is because they feel strongly that they should know. You may be familiar with the Japanese term 'ikigai', which has gained worldwide attention recently. Roughly translated as 'a reason for being', the concept further serves to remind us that it's wise to follow a career path and life that has meaning to us. It sounds wonderful and aspirational – unless we have no idea what would give our lives said meaning!

Here's your permission to stop feeling bad if you don't have a clear calling or purpose.

Meet Laura

Laura was made redundant from her job as Strategic Director of an innovation consultancy as soon as the UK went into its first Covid lockdown. While she was furloughed she started doing a bit of freelance work with the social enterprise United Edge, which focuses on social and environmental justice.

One day she was on a call in which everyone introduced themselves and explained what they did. Their answers varied from helping with hurricane relief to helping to prevent human trafficking. When asked what she did, she didn't much like her own answer, which was essentially "helping the growth of western capitalist brands". In a nutshell she felt like she wasn't doing enough, and in fact was inadvertently contributing to the climate crisis, which she felt was creating suffering on the other side of the world.

Right there and then she made a pledge to herself to make a difference and leave a legacy to be proud of. She wanted to be able to look her kids in the eye one day and say that she did all she could to mitigate climate change. She now ploughs her time and boundless energy into helping businesses and individuals become more aware of the effect they have on the environment. Amongst many other achievements, she is now an assessor at the Institute for

Sustainable Leadership at Cambridge University, has become a member of the 'Million Tree Pledge' and has delivered a TEDx talk on 'Facing climate change as a parent'.

Improved lifestyle

You're innocently scrolling through your social media feed when a post catches your attention. The author of the post, pictured smiling on a beach, is doing a great job of seducing you with stories of how wonderful life is as a 'digital nomad' and that you can also achieve a magnificent life of working two days a week while sipping mojitos on a beach in Costa Rica.

This may be an extreme version of the lifestyle you're aspiring to, or perhaps it's not. The point is that you are disillusioned by what your current working life looks like, and crave a lifestyle that is much more in line with what you're dreaming of. One of my clients expressed his desire simply and succinctly as "just wanting a nicer, easier life".

Working 12+ hours per day, eating at least one of our meals in front of a screen, not seeing and enjoying the company of the people we love and getting our kicks from alcohol, drugs, overeating, buying stuff we don't need and endlessly scrolling through social media has become the norm for many. Is it any wonder then, that the lure of a 'nicer' lifestyle is so strong?

Freedom

Freedom means different things to different people. What it means to you will most likely be completely different to your colleague, neighbour, partner, best friend or a prisoner of war. To you, it may mean working at the time of day that you're at your best. If your most productive time is 7pm-midnight, having to stick to a rigid nine-to-five will be stifling. It may mean being able to attend your child's school plays and sports days without having to ask for time off or feeling guilty for doing so. It may mean being able to work from a beachside cafe in Mexico for three months a year. It may mean working only a handful of hours a week. Whatever it means to you, a sense of freedom could be the main reason you're looking to quit your job.

The opportunity to make more money

The lure of earning more money can be a strong motivator. More money to improve your lifestyle, to buy a bigger house, to take care of your loved ones, to retire earlier.

Finding a new job or indeed a whole new career can seem like the most obvious way to reach your financial goal, whatever it may be.

Meet Simon

Simon worked for a paper distribution company for several years. He'd worked his way up from a manual role in the warehouse to eventually managing all 50 warehouse staff. He enjoyed his job and was good at it. A year before he quit, he got married, his wife had a baby shortly afterwards, and they made the decision that his wife would stay home to raise their son. It soon became apparent that what had been a decent salary when he was a bachelor, wasn't going to suffice with two extra mouths to feed. He'd had several conversations with his boss about increasing his salary, none of which had led to the outcome he was looking for. Simon, by then, knew the industry and its key players pretty well. Crucially, he also knew just how much profit the business was making! Spurred on by his new and incredibly supportive wife, Simon took the leap and set up a rival business. Within six months he'd secured enough contracts to earn what he'd been earning previously, and within two years he was "earning more money than I knew what to do with".

Fulfil your potential or lifelong dream

Have you always had the dream of being a full-time painter, an actor, author, business owner? Do you feel like you have something to offer the world that you can't deliver whilst in your nine-to-five, or whatever hours you normally do? Do people keep telling you that you should be a stand-up comedian or a singer? What's that thing you secretly, or indeed very openly, wish you could be spending your days doing? Many of us harbour a desire to do something for a living that feels more like a fun hobby than an endless chore.

Meet Michael

After 30 years of working in the same industry, Michael finally left his job working for Formula 1, taking a leap of faith and setting up his own coffee business. He had been thinking about roasting coffee since he was in his early twenties. His father's response at the time was "don't be so bloody stupid, boy! You've got yourself a good job; stick with it!". Assuming his father was right, Michael put his dream on hold.

However, the thought of running his own coffee business never left, and a couple of decades later, he finally invested every penny he had into setting up Golden Sheep Coffee and is now reaping the rewards.

"It got to a point in my life where I thought, 'If I don't do it, it's something I'll always regret.'"

You have an amazing business idea

This is a motivation that is very dear to my heart, as I'm someone who has a lot of business ideas and loves taking ideas from concept to reality. If you have an idea that you just can't stop thinking about, that gives you a fire in your belly and keeps you awake at night, for all the *right* reasons, then feel free to take this book as your rather oversized permission slip to JUST DO IT. Start a side hustle or take a leap of faith and go all in. If not now, then when?

You have a passion for something

Next time you find yourself in the company of a small gathering of people and the conversation is somewhat dry, why not liven things up and ask what they are passionate about.

Asking someone what they feel passionate about will often result in them having a minor seizure while racking their brains to come up with something worthy of posing as their so-called passion.

If you're lucky enough to be able to answer quickly and succinctly, you're in the minority. I'll hazard a guess that by picking up, or being given, this book, you would love nothing more than to be doing work that revolves around your passions. It could be a cause you feel particularly enthusiastic about, or a skill that when used makes all time seemingly evaporate.

Seeking equilibrium

Whatever your motivation, I'd like to plant a seed in your brain right now. Life is a beautiful mix of plans and accidents.

Too much planning and you don't leave any gaps for those awe-inspiring things that happen when you least expect them. Isn't it wonderful when you embark on that completely spontaneous weekend away, just because you felt like a mini adventure at the very last second? Or that last-minute invitation to an awesome party? Or that polite request to get involved in a really cool event?

Too many accidents, and over time you become the 'victim', because life just happens to you without you taking enough control over what you want it to look like. If you've found yourself endlessly complaining about your situation to anyone who'll listen, then I'm sorry to tell you that you have fallen into the victim trap. The victim blames everyone. Their boss, mother, partner, politicians. They blame everyone but themselves for their situation. If they're not blaming other people for their misfortunes, it's the weather, the economy, the state of modern society, discrimination, the political situation or undesirable advances in technology.

Like most things in life, we're looking for balance, some kind of equilibrium. Yes, do the planning, and yes, leave room for awesome surprises. We're aiming for a perfectly synchronised dance between the two. The big question is, which bits of your career do you want to have control over and which bits are you happy to leave to chance?

If you don't design your career path for yourself, someone else will do it for you, and there's a good chance you won't like their idea of what your path should look like. Is your employer really, truly, deeply invested in your happiness and fulfilment, or do they mostly care about your productivity? Does your spouse want you to feel energised by your work, or do they just want to be able to go on four overseas holidays every year?

Do you want life to happen to you, or do you want to grab the bull by the horns, and create the best goddamn career path and life you can possibly imagine for yourself and your loved ones? This could be your sliding doors moment. The moment you make a life-changing decision. Let's ensure you make it a good one!

Why you haven't quit yet

Resistance to change

Ah, the fascinating phenomenon of human resistance to change! We're all familiar with it to some extent. While we may consider ourselves adaptable creatures, and we marvel at progress and innovation around us, there's a peculiar attachment to the familiar that tends to persist. We don't like uncertainty. Our brains, wired for efficiency, prefer the tried-and-true over the unknown. It's not our fault. It's a little quirk that stems from our primal instincts to ensure our survival on this planet.

Some people love change, thrive on it, and would be utterly bored without aspects of their lives changing constantly. I say 'aspects of' because even those who adore nothing more than a moveable feast cling to the comfort and predictability of certain things. It could be the place they live, the partner they're with, their favourite t-shirt or the brand of tea they drink.

For others, change can be downright daunting. They generally find comfort in routine, clinging to what they know, like a cosy blanket on a rainy day. So the fact that you've been resistant to making a change in your career is just your evolutionary programming kicking in.

Why exactly is it that we're so inherently resistant to change?

It's all about that comfort zone we cherish. Many of us love routine and familiarity. We find solace in the predictable patterns of our daily lives. We fear the uncertainty that change brings, unsure of what lies beyond our familiar boundaries. Things are okay, and if you make a change you have something to lose.

We're hardwired to detect threats, and change often triggers that ancient alarm system. Our minds are brilliant at conjuring up worst-case scenarios. Our imaginations run wild, and we convince ourselves that change is the harbinger of doom.

Our brains have a nifty trick up their sleeves. You see, our neural pathways develop through repetition, forming well-worn paths like footprints on a beach. When change comes knocking, it means forging new pathways and abandoning the familiar ones. It's like asking our brain to navigate an uncharted jungle. No wonder it puts up a fight!

There's a formula!

You may be familiar with a change formula that was developed back in 1987 by the organisational theorists Richard Beckhard and Reuben T Harris:

Dissatisfaction x Vision x First Steps > Resistance to Change

It was really developed to help organisations identify the factors required for a successful transformation to occur and to analyse the likelihood of its success. However, over the years people have applied it to personal change too. I often refer to it with clients, and more often than not it strikes a chord and opens up fascinating insights into their particular reasons for resisting change.

The premise of Beckhard and Harris' theory is that in order for you to stop resisting change you need to feel a certain level of dissatisfaction with your current situation, you have to have a clear vision of what you want to do, and you have to take some kind of action to create momentum.

While this formula does provide an 'aha' moment for many, variations of it ring true for others.

You might identify with one of these variations:

Motivation x First Steps > Resistance to Change
Vision x Support x Time > Resistance to Change
Time x Motivation x Fears > Resistance to Change
Fears x Support x Vision > Resistance to Change
Dissatisfaction x Support > Resistance to Change
Vision x (a really) Good Reason (to want the change) x First Steps > Resistance to Change
Limiting Beliefs x Support x Vision > Resistance to Change
Faith x Support x Time > Resistance to Change

Let's explore some of these factors in more detail.

You're just not unhappy enough

You may be a little bit unhappy in your current role. But your dissatisfaction hasn't hit the level where it actively contributes to the push you need to make a change. In other words, there's a tipping point in your level of dissatisfaction, which could be triggered by your boss being particularly unreasonable one day. It could be that you've worked your little bottom off, asked for a rise in salary to reflect your contribution, and been knocked back.

If your dissatisfaction levels are currently below the tipping point and things are 'okay', there's every chance you'll stay exactly where you are. Then the only real decision you have to make is whether or not you will change your attitude towards your current situation. Will you continue to bore everyone to tears with endless moaning about how awful your job is, or will you put your best foot forward and approach work with a positive mindset?

Lack of vision

"I'm really unhappy in my job, but I just don't know what I should do instead."

Sound familiar?

In all likelihood, where your motivation to make a change in your work situation revolves around avoiding a current negative situation, a lack of vision could be the culprit for keeping you in a state of paralysis. You're lacking a vision of what you would be doing instead. Of how you'd be spending your days. Of how you'd be making an income.

Having a compelling vision motivates and guides personal change. It also propels us to take action. If this resonates with you, don't despair, this book is designed to help you get clear on your vision.

> *"It is never too late to be what you might have been."*
>
> — GEORGE ELIOT

First steps

So you're clear on why you want to quit your job and make a change, but you haven't actually taken any action other than reading this book – which is an excellent first step by the way!

You're procrastinating. We've all procrastinated on things at some point in our lives. We like the idea of going to the gym, maybe even take out an expensive membership, but then we don't actually go. We want to get eight hours of sleep every night, but end up watching mindless TV until the early hours. We want to start a side hustle, but would rather just think about it instead of taking action.

In other words, we're often great at coming up with ideas of things we'd like to do – less good at making them happen.

The reason for this is that somehow our brain has tricked us into believing that taking action is going to be more 'painful' than doing nothing, so we choose to avoid the pain. Our brain is focused very much on the short-term pain rather than the long-term gain we're likely to derive. It's a survival mechanism of sorts.

If you're going to make a change, it is absolutely going to feel a little bit uncomfortable, at least in the short-term. Incidentally, it won't feel nearly as uncomfortable as being stuck in a job that's making you miserable.

Baby steps are still steps

How many times have you heard someone complain about their current situation? They're overweight, they don't like where they live, they're always broke despite a good income, they don't have enough time to do things they enjoy.

I'll never forget something a close friend said to me many years ago when, embarrassingly, I'd fallen into the trap of complaining about something constantly. Hey, we're all human! She turned to me and with all the compassion and kindness in the world she uttered these seven words that are now imprinted in my brain: "If you don't like it, change it."

That doesn't mean you have to take massive action that blows up everything you know overnight. No! But you *do* have complete control over the changes you make in your life. The first step you take can be a baby step. Taking that first step is imperative to change.

> *"A journey of a thousand miles begins with a single step."*
>
> LAO TZU

It's not a priority

If there was a prize for burying your head in the sand and hoping that something will magically happen for everything to just fall into place, you'd be winning that prize right now. You wouldn't be the sole recipient of the prize however.

Most of us are overwhelmed by our everyday commitments to our families, friends, hobbies, household chores and work. So putting yourself and your needs first just doesn't seem like enough of a priority. It may feel far too self-indulgent and selfish to pursue your dream career.

There is also a tendency to prioritise things that give us short-term gratification, where we can see tangible results quickly without too much effort. So even doing the laundry can feel more rewarding than spending time strategising our career paths, because we see almost instant results for our effort with the former.

We instinctively know that spending time working out a career plan that is likely going to be hugely fulfilling in the long-term, will almost certainly require a much bigger investment of your time and brainpower than watching another episode of your favourite TV show.

What are you waiting for? Here is your virtual tap on the shoulder to make yourself and your career your priority – for as long as it takes for work to feel fun and meaningful to you again.

Lack of time

People in the UK who work full-time, spend an average of 37 hours per week at work. When you throw in family commitments, the commute, a bit of sleep, walking the dog, exercise and time for Netflix, it's easy to see why a lot of people feel like they don't have time to explore their career options. We're in a perpetual state of busyness. We're on auto-pilot, simply getting through the never ending to-do list and staying on top of our inboxes. We don't find the time to dedicate to thinking constructively about our careers.

(Beliefs) It's all in what you believe to be true

Beliefs are funny old things. Broken down, beliefs are simply thoughts that we keep on thinking. They are the stories we tell ourselves repeatedly.

But where do these beliefs and thoughts even come from?

Many of them come from our experiences and our environment. We are especially impressionable in childhood and absorb everything we hear, see and feel like sponges. All our experiences influence us and our beliefs in some way. The highs, the lows. The successes, the failures. The rejections, the jubilations.

Our beliefs can also be based on other people's experiences. They come from what other people have told us. The books we've read. The films we've watched. What our teacher told us in primary school. Crucially, many of our beliefs about ourselves and the world at large come from what our parents have taught and shown us by example, particularly before the age of seven. No pressure at all on those of us who are parents!

For years we've been warned that "that's not safe", "that's not realistic", "that's not cool", "that's not achievable for you".

We live by a list of 'shoulds'. I *should* go for that promotion. I *should* earn more money. I *should* stick with a job I don't like. I *should* wait till I retire to be happy. I *should* make my parents proud. In short, we subconsciously create a long list of limiting beliefs that stop us from achieving things. How many times have you talked yourself out of following a dream before you've seriously explored how you could make your dream a reality? How many times have you created limitations for yourself? These limitations are mostly self-imposed.

We don't often challenge or logically dispute our own beliefs. But beliefs are 100 per cent optional, and rewiring our belief systems is completely possible. We don't have to believe everything we think. Upgraded beliefs always lead to upgraded results. Your beliefs are absolutely crucial because they will determine your current and ongoing success. Can you be open to the possibility that your current beliefs around your career might not be serving you?

Whose beliefs have you caught along the way? Whose beliefs are you still catching? Whose beliefs do you regurgitate without really thinking about whether they truly resonate with you? Crucially, are your beliefs serving you in your quest to do work that is meaningful to you? Which ones are holding you back?

> *"Whether you think you can or you can't you're probably right."*
>
> HENRY FORD

Are you open to having some fun with beliefs? If you believed some of the most ridiculous things that you've been told about yourself, what would your top four be?

Here are mine:

- You're not clever enough to go to university (my primary school teacher, when I was about seven years old).
- You're not very academic (my A-level Art teacher).
- What a stupid girl you are (someone very close to me, whom I won't name).
- You haven't really got the stamina to run your own business (a supposed mentor when I set up my first business).

Frankly, I'm surprised I've not needed years of therapy to overcome these beliefs that others tried to instill in me!

There's a possibility that I believed them at some point in my life. But they also gave me a fire in my belly to prove that the beliefs they held about me were complete and utter rubbish. But what if I had been told those things repeatedly, and had taken them to be true? How different my life would look now. There's a good chance I wouldn't have even bothered applying to universities, never mind graduating with a BSc from one of the top universities in the UK. And I almost certainly wouldn't have had the courage to set up multiple businesses – or write this book.

> *"The only thing that's keeping you from getting what you want is the story you keep telling yourself."*
>
> TONY ROBBINS

Try this

1. List the beliefs about yourself, your career and the world at large that have got you to where you are today.
2. What belief or beliefs do you have that are currently stopping you from going after your dream career?
3. Where do these beliefs come from?
4. What new and upgraded beliefs could you replace those limiting beliefs with? What beliefs would serve you in your quest? If you could believe anything you want about yourself, what would that new belief be?
5. What evidence do you have to back this belief up with?

When we accept that some of our beliefs could be tweaked or completely changed so that they serve us rather than hold us back, then major shifts can start to happen. However, it's futile to expect that we can change our deep-rooted beliefs overnight. It will take time, and it will take willingness on your part to work on creating beliefs that will support you in your quest to your dream career.

Meet Sarah

Sarah grew up on a council estate near Barnsley, UK. Her father, who was arguably the biggest influence on her early career, had all the best intentions when he encouraged her to find and stay in a stable job. He had worked for the local council all his life.

So you'd be forgiven for assuming that Sarah's beliefs around her career and what she might be capable of achieving were very much shaped by an early age, and never changed.

Sarah adopted a 'growth mindset' however. Embarking on a journey of self-discovery, she surrounded herself with all the self-development books she could get her hands on, and sought out coaches and mentors.

When she, like many others, lost her job as a result of Covid, she found the courage to take on contract roles and within a year built a six-figure project management consultancy, something she never dreamed she'd be capable of. "If you think that there's something out there that you want to do, that you want to achieve, no one's gonna achieve it for you. You've got to go for it. You've got to live that life yourself."

Fears

> *"Courage comes by being brave; fear comes by holding back."*
>
> PUBLILIUS SYRUS

The thing that holds most people back from following their dream career is of course fear. Fear of failure, fear of the unknown, fear of success (yes, there is such a thing!), fear of being judged or even worse ridiculed.

The good news is that feeling fearful is totally normal. The fear we experience is our brain's way of trying to keep us safe, and as that is our brain's number 1 job, we won't hold that against it. Most of us are hardwired to stay in our comfort zone, where the world is safe and predictable.

If you are a parent or have spent any amount of time with young kids, you'll know that we have an inbuilt instinct to keep them safe. We repeatedly issue instructions for them to "be careful" and "don't touch that" in an attempt to keep them from harm.

Our brain is doing exactly the same thing. By sending us warning signals when we so much as contemplate a change, it's attempting to keep us safe.

Here are some fears you may have been experiencing.

Fear of being judged

"Have you heard that Beth is setting up a gardening business? As if she knows the first thing about running a business… or gardening for that matter! I give it six months!"

Conversations like this might go on behind your back when you share your dreams. When I told a close friend I was setting up my career coaching business, he was quick to remind me that he had very recently completed a career coaching qualification and quizzed me on when I had qualified as a coach (2005, if you're interested!). I felt the fact that I'd qualified as a coach and had been coaching people on and off for almost two decades didn't count for much in his eyes. I'm not proud to admit that I let it affect me. For a few days after our conversation I felt judged, and not in a good way.

If you're worried about what other people will think of you and your desire to make a big career move, you're not alone. The fear of being judged, or FOPO (fear of other people's opinion) is hardwired in most of us. We're social creatures and have a primal need to connect with one another. Hence our strong desire to fit in. This desire and fear of the contrary is ingrained in us from a time when being expelled from your tribe was a matter of life and death because your chances of survival on your own were slim to none.

That's why simply telling yourself "who cares what anyone else thinks?!" is rarely enough. As drastic as it may sound, when we feel alienated from our tribe we can feel a lack of ability to survive.

Having said all of that, I'd like you to be open to the possibility that no one is actually judging you. And if they are, their judgement will likely not last as long as it takes you to eat a burrito. Most people are far too busy obsessing about themselves than to give what you're up to more than two minutes thought.

If they are indeed judging you, they are doing so for a couple of reasons:

- They are jealous that you are following your dream. They wish they could be following theirs, but are too scared and are therefore taking the much much easier option of ridiculing your bold ambitions.
- Talking badly about you is making them feel better about themselves. It's a direct reflection of their own perceived self-worth. Making negative judgement on what you're doing shows that they have unresolved internal struggles. May I be so bold as to suggest you gift them a copy of this book!

You'll never get support and approval from absolutely everyone you know. So if you're going to focus on just a few people's opinions, it's worth considering whose opinion *actually* matters to you. There will be people who pass judgement no matter what. How much are you willing to let this affect you?

The best thing you can do is to get your act together, show up with confidence, follow your dreams and prove to everyone just how happy you can be in your work.

Ditch the victim mentality that is keeping you stuck, and assume the role of the creator. It's a heck of a lot more fun and empowering. If you knew for sure that you could get people to believe brilliant things about you, what would they be? How can you start to shape people's opinion of you in the most positive way?

Fear of the unknown

When we're fearful of the unknown our clever little brains will come up with a million different reasons (some may call them excuses) not to follow through on our plans. Hopefully this book is already making you think about things slightly differently.

Sometimes our fears are totally justified and I'm certainly not encouraging completely reckless behaviour. But often we have irrational fears that stop us from doing things that are important to us. At times, we have to feel the fear and do it anyway.

When your faith is greater than the fear of the unknown, you'll find you can move metaphorical mountains and achieve what seemed impossible. You don't know what you're capable of until you take the first step into the abyss and try something new.

Are you ready to have a bit of fun exploring your fears and playing around with them so they hold less power over you? Good, let's do it!

Try this

Ways you can overcome your fears:

- Politely thank your fears for attempting to keep you safe.
- Write down each of your fears and talk them through with someone you trust, who will not judge you and will gently help you challenge them and their validity.
- Consider what the worst-case scenario would be if you quit your job to pursue something your heart desires, and it doesn't work out.

Can you make peace with the worst-case scenario? How much worse is your worst-case scenario than your current scenario?*
- What can you do to prevent your fears from coming true?
- What are you willing to compromise to follow your dream career?
- What's the likely cost of your inaction?
- What will happen if you stay in your job for the next six months, two years, 20 years?
- How does the thought of staying in the same job for the next 20 years make you feel?

*clients often have a huge 'aha' moment when they realise that they are currently already living a life that is their worst-case scenario.

If all else fails, you may like to watch the Pixar movie *Luca* to witness one of the protagonists tell Luca to use the simple mantra "Silenzio Bruno!" whenever he feels fear. Bruno being the name he gives his fearful mind. It's sweet, it's simple and it's effective. Try it!

Money

> *"Your wealth is your life experience, not your money."*
>
> JOHN COLLEE

I challenge you to find a topic that is more emotive, divisive, challenging, fear-inducing than money. It has the potential to be more taboo than sex, religion and politics all rolled into one. It's also cited as the number one reason people feel they are unable to make a career change. Many of us have complicated, deep-rooted associations and beliefs around money. The pursuit of it is deeply ingrained in us, not merely because we need it to meet our basic needs for food and shelter, but also because it affords us a certain lifestyle.

Many years ago, in my first corporate job at Motorola, I was attending our annual distributor conference in Madrid in a very lovely hotel. Over a delicious dinner with matching wines for every course, I was chatting to one of our distributors. Let's call him Karl. Karl was in his late 50s and had done rather well for himself financially over the years.

He spent most of the evening telling me in great detail about how successful he'd been and evidenced his success by telling me about all the properties he now owned in glamorous locations across the world. I have to admit that my 24-year-old self was in awe.

However I was also curious, and the conversation took a very sudden and unexpected turn. As someone who had lived in too many places to call anywhere 'home', I was genuinely intrigued to know where *he* called home. Two decades after this conversation I still remember vividly the dramatic change in his body language. His shoulders, which had only seconds earlier been pushed back with pride, slumped in an instant. In one foul swoop he went from being super confident, verging on cocky, to looking like a little lost school boy. With sadness in his eyes, he considered my question carefully before answering sombrely that he supposed since the breakdown of his marriage he didn't really know where home was anymore. He said he just tried to be near his grown-up kids and grandkids as much as possible. What had been a bragging session went to what felt like a therapy session. I felt genuinely sorry for someone who just moments earlier had seemed so inspirational.

Yes, he was successful in monetary terms, but was he really living a full life? It seemed that he wasn't. Our conversation taught me a very valuable lesson at a young age. I vowed to myself that I would be very mindful of what I chased, and what I defined as success. For me the lesson was clear. Money on its own is futile and worthless. It's only truly valuable if you have people you love who you can share it with.

Daniel Ek, founder of Spotify, isn't shy to share with the world that he fell into depression following the sale of his business Advertigo for $1.25 million when he was just 23. He found himself surrounded by people who were drawn to him because of his business success.

"They were people who were there for the good times, but if it ever turned ugly they'd leave me in a heartbeat. I had always wanted to belong and I had been thinking that this was going to get solved when I had money, and instead I had no idea how I wanted to live my life."

I love asking people what they would do if they suddenly had enough money to never have to work again. They could fill their days just doing things that make them feel happy, energised and fulfilled.

Honestly, most people don't know.

It's quite bizarre that most of us lack the imagination to dream up a life that stretches very far beyond the life we're already leading and is familiar to us.

We spend a massively disproportionate amount of time thinking and worrying about the pursuit of money, and very little on how we would actually spend it. Doesn't really make much sense. But we're human, and we do loads of things that don't make much sense when we stop to think about them.

Conversely, ask someone who *has* spent time thinking about exactly what they'd do if they didn't have to make a living. Then witness them light up while they regale you with their dreams and aspirations. It's really fun to witness. Why not become one of them?

There's no getting away from the fact that money, and our beliefs around it, will have a massive effect on our career decisions. It's no coincidence that many people embark on their career transition when they have a cash windfall such as a redundancy or inheritance. Having a financial buffer takes the pressure off and allows for a degree of freedom to explore options. An abundance of money certainly gives us more control over how we spend our time.

The two main limiting beliefs around money and career transition that come up regularly are:

1. I will probably make less money in my new career.
2. I have to continue to earn *at least* the same amount of money as I do now.

Do either of those ring true for you? Let's explore them.

I will probably make less money in my new career

Many people hold the belief that a change in career will make them less well off financially. Sometimes this is true – at least in the short-term while you go through a period of retraining or re-establishing yourself. Sometimes it's a matter of making peace with the fact that there's a good chance your long-term earning potential will be curtailed.

However, the opposite can also be true. The examples of people who left secure jobs to go on to make significantly more money are endless. If you open your eyes and ears to them, you'll find plenty of stories of people who have gone on to earn considerably more after taking a leap of faith.

Can you find role models who are earning what you would like to earn in your chosen field?

I have to continue to earn *at least* the same amount of money as I do now

If your current job earns you just about enough money to get by, then this is a very real concern. There's no getting away from the fact that we all need money to survive in this world, unless you take the highly unconventional path of becoming completely self-sufficient.

How much is enough?

Many of us are obsessed with the desire to earn more money without consciously deciding how much is 'enough' for us. Bringing a specific figure to our awareness enables us to strive for it and increases the chance that we'll then feel satisfied when we achieve it. This doesn't mean to say you aren't open to earning more, but anything above the figure you've established is the cherry on top. The alternative that many of us experience is that we can't get off the hedonic treadmill, which gives us the constant niggling feeling that we could or should be earning more.

Our self-worth

It's easy to fall into the trap of feeling like our worth directly correlates with how much money we earn. Many of us hold the ardent belief that we should be paid what we're worth. However, on a logical level we probably know this to not be true. Who is the judge of how much your individual contribution is worth? Your boss? HR? If the amount of money we earnt were directly proportional to the value we provided, nurses would arguably earn significantly more than bankers. While we could argue that

that would be a much fairer way for the world to operate, it's unlikely that we'll ever see this playing out in reality.

What if, instead of attaching our self-worth to how much money we earn, how we look or how many social media followers we have, we focus on how much joy we spread, or how many people's lives we touch and improve, or how much good we do in the world?

Spending money out of habit

Another trap many of us have fallen into is spending money on things that don't actually contribute anything positive to our lives for more than the time it takes to pay for it.

> *"We buy things we don't need, with money we don't have, to impress people we don't like."*
>
> DAVE RAMSEY

Has anyone on their deathbed ever said: "I just really wish I'd bought more *stuff*"?

We get caught up in a hamster wheel where we've forgotten what we're chasing because we've forgotten what's actually important to us. We're addicted to money and the idea of having more of it. So we work harder in jobs we hate in the hope that someday, somewhere along the line we'll have 'enough' to finally build our dream home, finally go on that wonderful holiday (which will only last two weeks by the way... and then you're back to reality), buy that fancy car, to retire comfortably, to *finally* be happy.

Except it doesn't work that way.

Everyone should be free to spend money on whatever they like. But too often we get into a habit of spending money that we don't need to, and that then forces us into a situation that has us assuming that we have to earn a certain amount of money to keep up our current lifestyle, to 'keep up with the Joneses'. If you're honest with yourself, and think about the things you have spent money on recently, there's a good chance that you bought them because you think they will give you respect and/or admiration, rather than fulfil an actual need.

We are creatures of habit. But we should never underestimate how adaptable we are. If you are indeed going to earn less than you've been accustomed to, then it might not be the hellish nightmare you envision it to be.

You may be familiar with the 'lifestyle creep' concept, which basically infers that as an individual's income rises, so do our spending habits, and what used to be 'luxuries' become the new 'necessities'. It's fun to spend money on luxuries, but the novelty wears off after a while, and so we keep chasing more and more extravagant luxuries in the hope they'll fill a void.

On the flip side, you might well find that you spend less on things that you don't actually need anyway, and feel *better* for it, not worse.

I'm not glamourising or advocating being poor by any means. If you have enough money, however, to take care of your basic needs, then maybe doing something you love doing can take priority over earning lots of money that you don't actually need.

Reducing our dependence on earning a certain amount of money can immediately take away the belief and burden that we must stay in a job that's making us unhappy. It affords us a bit of freedom, and can take a massive weight off our shoulders.

Would your loved ones prefer to have expensive things in their lives, or a parent, friend, partner, offspring who is happy and present with them? Of course, they're not mutually exclusive. If you are able to find a way to achieve both, you're on to something really special. Other people have done it, so it stands to reason that you can too.

Meet Susanne

Susanne worked her way up the corporate ladder in a multinational telecoms company. She led a very comfortable life that included plenty of holidays and going out for dinner and drinks without having to think much about the cost. However, things changed when she started to feel discontent with her career and didn't find her job as fun and challenging as she previously had.

She started to feel financially trapped in her job, and perhaps even her life. She and her husband had just put down an offer on a new house, which had meant taking out a bigger and more expensive mortgage. She recalls having a mild panic attack one day after work as she wasn't sure it was the right thing to do. She worried it would set her back years in terms of pursuing a new career.

She recalls not being able to shake off the feeling that she was too reliant on, and almost addicted to, having a big salary. "A big part of my identity was associated with being able to do what I wanted without having to worry about money. I knew I wanted to make a change but I was very dependent on my salary on a psychological level. I set myself a goal of having a certain amount of money saved and decided by that time I would leave my job and find something else – not knowing what that something else was yet."

True to her word, as soon as the goal had been met, she handed in her notice. "It was scary but I kept reminding myself that you rarely regret the things you do, only the things you don't.

"When I decided to resign from a very well-paid job I did it mostly to challenge myself to not be dependent on earning a certain amount of money. I was so focused on having challenges at work but maybe the challenge I really needed to take on was my relationship with money. I was also feeling more and more embarrassed by the amount of money I could squander away. Few people understood why I would give up such financial stability – was my job really that bad? No, I just didn't want to do it anymore and, actually, I did not need to justify that."

"I made a lot of money, but I also spent a lot of money."

After resigning she became frugal with her spending. While her husband was hugely supportive of her decisions, they weren't in a position where he could support the family on his own. She took a bit of time out to figure out what she wanted to do next. Knowing that she was interested in working with young people after being a mentor for the Prince's Trust in the past, she eventually went into teaching Business and Financial studies. Her first salary was about the same as her company car allowance had been in the corporate world. However, she absolutely thrived on the new challenges and the environment she was in.

It was intense work and at times she worked out that given how much time she put into it, she was barely receiving the minimum wage as she had to spend so much time getting to grips with the new role. But it was so rewarding, she no longer felt the desire to buy stuff to compensate for the fact she didn't really enjoy her job. And she was willing to give up most of the dinners out and the fancy holidays.

She told herself it was a choice, a choice she could easily reverse if she ever wanted to. "And I think that is a very powerful thing to tell yourself – it is a choice. My husband also changed careers and we went from a high-income household to just about managing to pay our bills month by month – by choice. Unlike others in society we had a choice so I count myself lucky. We scaled completely back and have then slowly introduced some of the luxuries we really enjoy. We also cut out the ones we didn't."

Much less concerned about projecting a certain financial status now, she doesn't mind telling friends that they won't be able to go out for dinner because they can't afford it, or are choosing to spend their money elsewhere. "Having the freedom to do the job I want for as long as I want is a lot more valuable to me."

Let's challenge some preconceptions and beliefs you have around money.

The first step is to take the time to look at your finances in detail. This will allow you to apply a solid level of logic to your career decisions, rather than basing them on emotions alone.

Some powerful questions to ask yourself are:

1. What are my fixed monthly expenses?
2. Where am I spending money unnecessarily?
3. How much money do I need/want to be earning to live my dream life? How much money is enough?
4. What is my earning potential in my new endeavour?
5. What are my long-term financial goals?
6. How much money, if any, do I need to invest in my career change?
7. How long can/am I happy to live off my savings for?

8. How will my earning potential in my new role affect those closest to me?
9. What are some ways I can supplement my income whilst in my career transition?

Safety net

If you are planning to make a drastic career change and the amount of money you're going to earn is likely to be less than you're accustomed to, it's worth having a safety net. Work out how much money you would need for changes to your income to feel less daunting.

Your identity – Who are you anyway?

Doing a similar, or even the same job, for a long time unsurprisingly leads to your identity being very heavily tied up to the work you do and the organisation you work for. People know you in a certain capacity. You have worked hard to become the manager, director, c-suite level executive. Your current role might come with perks, access to a certain network, and might allow you to travel business class wherever you go.

You have a reputation in your field. You have prestige. You are *somebody*! If you make a career change you may well be facing the possibility of becoming a *nobody*. There is a reason why people who retire are susceptible to tumbling into depression. Your identity and self-worth can be so intertwined with your career, that you can't even begin to imagine who you'd be without it. Who are you without your work? The thought of having to reinvent yourself may seem like a daunting and challenging prospect.

Meet Natasa

When co-founder of Wizz Air, Natasa gave up her career to move to Abu Dhabi and be with the love of her life, it took her several years of soul-searching, re-educating herself in completely new areas of interest and exploring her options to really find herself again. She felt like she'd left behind an important part of herself and what ensued was what she describes as the hardest period in her life and feeling like she was in a black hole. Because her partner Jim was often away with work, she frequently felt lonely and found that she didn't make a very good 'lady of leisure'. She found no satisfaction in the endless coffee mornings and the shopping afternoons.

"I was somebody important. And suddenly I'm moving to the Middle East, which was unknown territory for me. I was suddenly just a sidekick to a man there. So that was a difficult one, but ultimately it was the best thing that could have happened to me because everything that I unfolded from there really – reflecting back – justified that change... It was super hard, but absolutely the right decision."

Over time, she started to turn things around. She made new friendships, which she describes as being "on a different level", she discovered energy healing, studied positive leadership and strategy, and took up yoga.

In her bestselling book Ready for Takeoff, she says, "I wanted to feel good in my body again, be a better spouse for Jim and a vibrant and patient mother for our son Daniel".

Natasa and Jim have now joined forces to create a fantastic business which combines their vast experience in the corporate world with their passion for health and wellbeing.

Jim's story is equally as interesting, and you'll read more about him in Part 6.

Starting over

You've likely worked really hard, put in a lot of hours, and endured blood, sweat and tears to get to where you are today. So making a career change at this stage of your life can feel like you're starting over and the years you've spent building your career are going to waste. It can feel as though you've run 40km of a marathon, and now you're starting a new race, before you've passed the 42km finish line.

In fact, stepping into a new career demonstrates flexibility, adaptability, resilience and courage. What if you could view your career change as an evolution rather than a complete re-invention of yourself? Just like friendships, jobs can be "a reason, a season, or a lifetime" (Brian A. Chalker).

You think you're too old

A client once told me that when he was around 35 years old he'd spoken to his retired father about changing careers, and his father had rather harshly remarked that "you can't teach an old dog new tricks". Now aged 42, my client wished he hadn't taken his father's words to heart, as it then took him another six years to make the transition into what he now describes as his dream job.

If you keep thinking about quitting, and really can't find the joy in your current role anymore, then age should not be a barrier. There are no rules here! The way I see it: the older you get, the more reason you have to do something that's going to make you happy. Because every day you wake up, you're one day closer to not waking up.

Here are some of my favourite examples of people who have made audacious career changes later in life.

Julia Child: She began her career at the Office of Strategic Services, a government agency that would later become the CIA, where she helped to develop a shark repellent. When her husband's job took them to Paris, she enrolled in a cooking class at Le Cordon Bleu at the age of 37. This awakened a passion for French cuisine, which eventually led to her publishing the groundbreaking cookbook *Mastering the Art of French Cooking* at the age of 49. Her TV show *The French Chef* debuted two years later, making Julia one of the world's first 'celebrity chefs'.

Ronald Reagan: Perhaps one of the most famous career switches in recent history, actor Ronald Reagan was 54 when he announced he was running for governor of California in 1965. He went on to become the 40th president of the United States in 1981, at the age of 69.

When you're too set in your ways, even just the thought of having to reinvent yourself can be completely overwhelming. The world's most interesting people are the ones who have a growth mindset. That is to say, they have an endlessly open mind, are happy for their assumptions to be challenged, enjoy learning new things and having new experiences.

Meet Anthony

Anthony has a varied career history spanning more than four decades, but the common thread throughout his career has always been his passion for education and technology.

When both his and his wife's businesses took a turn for the worse during Covid lockdown and their incomes ceased almost overnight, they decided to bring their skill sets together. Anthony's wife Astrid had been a Jin Shin Jyutsu practitioner for many years, and with Anthony's expertise, they decided to take her business online. They developed her website and products, and within half a year they were back to earning the same as their combined income pre-Covid. Another six months later, they had quadrupled their income.

Having a business that is now fully online has opened up a host of opportunities for Anthony, not least being able to become a digital nomad at the age of 65. With glee, he told me that he never wakes up to the sound of an alarm clock anymore! "If I'm going to work for myself, I'm going to sleep for as long as my body needs to sleep."

As I write this, he has absolutely no intention of retiring any time soon because he's having far too much fun. "I don't think I'll ever retire. Retirement is not part of my success. There's still just so much to do. For as long as my brain is functioning, I'll forever be involved in learning new stuff."

You don't know what to do

If you've been in the same industry, in the same company, in the constant presence of the same people for years, it's not surprising that you've perhaps forgotten who you are and what brings you joy. It's easy to start believing that there is no joy to be found in work. It's just something you have to endure to keep bringing in the money so that you and your loved ones can continue to enjoy the lifestyle you've become accustomed to.

Let's explore who you really are and what makes you tick!

PART 3
(Re)discovering YOU

Finding the joy

If you are completely honest with yourself and think about what percentage of your working days you currently spend doing something that you really enjoy, what would your answer be?

Even if you believe that you are in the worst job you can possibly imagine, there is likely to be a tiny element of your work that brings you joy, regardless of whether you're conscious of it or not.

When you're in a job that is making you miserable it's incredibly easy to focus on all the things you hate about it. Your nagging boss, the endless commuting, your annoying co-workers, the crappy canteen food, your desk chair that squeaks every time you move. Fill in the blanks. You know better than anyone all the things you dislike about your job. Focusing on these things allows little, or indeed no, room for any positives.

Try this

My challenge to you is to start noticing the things that are positive in your workday, that spark joy and energise you. Even if they feel tiny and a little bit insignificant or trivial at first. Do you have a nice view from your office? Is one of your colleagues also one of your best friends outside of work? Do you receive recognition from your boss for a job well done? Does the coffee machine in your office spit out a really decent cup of decaf, double shot, caramel-infused macchiato?

All of these things are important to notice because they will start to lift your mood and attitude towards your current job immediately. A really great habit to get into is to write a few words at the end of each day, reflecting on the positives – the things that lit you up that day.

When you read back over them after a few days, weeks or months, can you find the common thread? Are you surprised by any of your findings?

Once you start to unearth the activities that fill you with joy and energy, explore how you may be able to incorporate more of those into your day, and less of the ones that drain you of all your energy and make you feel grumpy.

Not only does that ensure that you start to enjoy your current work situation slightly – or even a lot – more, it will also give you great insight into what activities your next job should ideally incorporate.

You can take back control over your career right now. It's time to start seeing yourself through a new, shinier lens. And the first step is to work out what activities feed your soul. When something 'feeds your soul', you feel an almost magical sensation of your heart leaping with joy. Your spirit does a little happy dance and you lose all concept of time.

Ideally you're aiming for a minimum of 80 per cent of the day-to-day activities in your working day to be enjoyable. There may be some people who love absolutely every aspect of their work, but I haven't come across too many of those. Most people who love their work still find themselves having to engage in some activities that don't make them jump for joy. Maybe that's not such a bad thing either. As the adage goes, you have to experience darkness to appreciate the light. So arguably, having to spend a bit of time on tasks that don't light your fire, may help to highlight the bits that do.

Here are some examples of how real people – my clients – describe the work they now so love:

- "It feels like heaven."
- "I get such a buzz from it."
- "I felt completely energised by doing…"
- "I can't describe the peace and contentment I feel when I'm working."
- "It's just the best feeling in the world."
- "I can't wait to wake up tomorrow and do it all over again."
- "I have so much energy."

You can imagine that one of my favourite things in the world is to listen to people talk with such enthusiasm about their work.

If you think this all sounds too happy clappy, new-age hippy for you, then it's possible you've been unhappy in your job for so long you have no idea what it feels like to enjoy work anymore. Misery often leads to scepticism and cynicism.

The good news is that if you spend some time on the pursuit, I guarantee you will start to find things that you're passionate about again.

Remember who you are?

> *"Can you remember who you were, before the world told you who you should be?"*
>
> CHARLES BUKOWSKI

I'll bet that you know some of those people who appear to have been born knowing exactly what they were put on this earth to do. They are passionate about, and fully dedicated to, their calling. They've never questioned whether they're on the right path. They just know that they are. When asked what he would have done for a living if he hadn't been a professional football player, Thierry Henry replied nonchalantly that he would have been an "amateur football player".

Monsieur Henry is, however, in the minority. If *you* are absolutely clear what you're passionate about, *you* are also in the minority.

The advice that you should "follow your passions" more often than not invokes an overwhelming sense of anxiety in people. This is because if you ask most people what they're passionate about they're unable to give an immediate and succinct answer. Most of us don't sit around thinking about what we're passionate about. If you are someone who doesn't instinctively know what you're passionate about, I recommend not panicking. Instead, bask in the newfound knowledge that you are not alone, and then start rediscovering little things that make you feel happy. Rediscover what you love to spend your time doing. Get to know yourself again. If you were dating a new potential life partner, how would you go about getting to know them? You'd probably ask them lots of questions. You'd *really* listen to their answers. You'd spend quality time with them. What do you need to do to get to know the real you again? In the words of the singer James Morrison, you're "not lost, just undiscovered".

Somewhere along the way we forgot what makes us happy. Over the years we've lost ourselves in our work, in our relationships, our families, the hamster wheel, in making other people happy, or fulfilling their expectations of us.

There's a very good chance that you had much more of a clue of what career would make you really happy when you were four or five years old. Before you started school, and before teachers and parents started to notice, and point out, all the things you *weren't* good at, and tried to rectify that. Sadly, it's not uncommon for kids to spend so long trying, or being forced, into learning things that they have absolutely no interest in that they ultimately lose interest in learning all together. Our love of learning and being curious may well have been beaten out of us at a very young age.

Then you hit your teenage years and likely did just what your peers were doing. You did what was considered cool and hid away the parts of you that were different and uncool. You tried to fit in as much as possible, thereby dimming a light inside you that would have burnt bright if it had been given half the chance.

Is it any wonder then that a huge number of us simply follow a path of least resistance, at least in terms of self-actualisation, and end up in jobs which make us question our mere existence? We get to middle age and wonder how the heck we've ended up in a job that we don't enjoy, and often even hate.

For many people Covid came as a big wakeup call, as well as an opportunity to take time to reflect on our lives and what matters most to us. Perhaps you were one of them. For the first time in living memory the whole world was forced to stop. Many of us found ourselves with more time on our hands than we'd ever known what to do with. Suddenly we weren't jumping on the daily commuter train at some ungodly hour and returning home only once the kids were tucked up and fast asleep. It was the first time in our adult lives that we weren't constantly rushing around. Covid gave us time to reflect, and what we saw in that reflection came as a harsh reality check.

If Covid wasn't your time to stop and reflect, then perhaps now is. Contrary to popular belief, you don't need a global pandemic to take stock of your life.

Try this

Ask your friends, family and/or people who know you well:

- What do you think I'm better at than most people?
- What did I do as a child that was slightly, or very, unusual?
- What captured my imagination?
- What did I spend my spare time doing when I was left to my own devices?
- What makes me slightly quirky?
- If you had to describe me to someone, which three to five adjectives would you use?
- What do you think are my best traits?

Meet Danny

It was just another day when, while on his way to a client meeting, Danny suddenly lost all feeling from the waist down. His speech had also gone, and it wasn't until afterwards he realised that he had had a serious nervous breakdown. There had been several signs he'd been heading that way, but he'd been so focused on delivering on his work that he'd ignored them all.

His physical breakdown was the catalyst for making a big change. He was forced to make the life-changing decision of whether to stick with a very well-paid job, or make a bold career move and take a step into the unknown.

It took him a few months to recover and while he was in limbo – living at a friend's house – asking himself what he was interested in, he couldn't think of anything. One day while doodling on a notepad, his wife said, "I remember you saying that you wanted to do something like graphic design when you were at school. Why don't you do that?" Something clicked for him in that instant. His response was "okay", like all he had been waiting for was a little nudge in the right direction.

The rest, as they say, is history. He started creating designs for people, and within a few months he'd built a business that not only provided a new income stream but, more importantly, gave him the opportunity to spend his days doing what he truly loved to do.

Your unique blend

Be yourself, everyone else is taken.

I'm sure you've seen this inspirational, motivational, well-meaning quote on t-shirts, mugs, your Instagram feed and maybe even a billboard or two.

I don't think anyone can dispute the fact that we're all unique. But what's the point of obsessing about the fact that you're unique? How does that help you? Is it just a nice thing to say to make you feel special?

As it turns out, when it comes to doing work you love, it's pretty vital.

Your life experiences, the family you were born into, the environment you grew up in, the friends and contacts you made along the way, your experiences within the work environment, and your interests outside of work play a huge role in creating a unique view of the world. And it's precisely that view that is invaluable… if you tap into it.

I like to call the amalgamation of our experiences, interests and skills our 'unique blend'.

We tend to take our own experiences and uniqueness for granted, hence our unique blend is often massively underrated and underappreciated. It's not always obvious to us how our unique blend can lead to a rich and fulfilling career if exploited. Intellectually, we know our experiences, interests and skills have shaped who we are, but we don't often stop to reflect on this, and on how we can use this unique mix to our advantage.

Becoming aware of, tapping into and ultimately capitalising on our unique blend equips us with a huge competitive advantage when applying for our next dream job; looking to further our career within our existing organisation; or starting a new business from scratch. It can also boost our confidence simply knowing that we bring something truly unique to a role. A rare angle or extraordinary insight that no one else could bring to the party.

Alli Webb, founder of Dry Bar, who sold her business in 2019 for $255 million puts it beautifully: "I really believe everything I did in my life uniquely prepared me to sit at the helm of a blow dry empire."

What are the things that you're naturally drawn to or really good at? And what unique experiences have you had that you take for granted, but could contribute to your unique blend?

Here are some examples of not-immediately-obvious things that could contribute to your unique blend. Some, you'll notice, are things that could seem negative from the outset, but we all know that our biggest learnings come from our biggest challenges. In life you either win or you learn. Perhaps they'll spark some ideas for you:

- That year you lived in Paris
- Your experience of captaining the hockey team at school
- The fact that you're fascinated by architecture
- Your fabulous sense of humour
- Your amazing organisational skills
- Your love of technology
- Being diagnosed with ADHD
- Your Italian heritage
- Your public school education

- Being rejected by the love of your life
- Being a parent
- Being the child of an immigrant
- Having no qualifications beyond your GCSEs

Your superpowers

Did you know that Paul McCartney had no idea he had any musical talent until he left full-time education? He even applied to sing with the Liverpool Cathedral choir and got rejected!

There's every chance that you have one or two superpowers up your sleeve that you haven't had the opportunity to discover, explore and revel in yet. Very often our superpowers lie in the wondrous combination of things that we're really good at and enjoy doing.

Passion + Talent = Superpower

Can you sell snow to a snowman? Does the room go completely silent, and do you get everyone's full attention when you give a presentation? Perhaps mentoring a younger, less experienced staff member is your thing. Maybe you love nothing more than writing up a report. Is it working out a new and more efficient process for something laborious?

Start noticing and making a note of these things. Consider every day a new opportunity to recognise what you love and are good at. The key to ensuring you find joy in your work is discovering, fostering and using these skills and turning them into your superpower.

Is your 'weakness' actually your biggest strength?

Throughout my early career I was plagued by the belief that I had this rather undesirable trait of starting, but never finishing, things. I've always found it extremely easy to get caught up in the excitement of a new project or business – mine and other people's.

Once something reaches the status quo however, my interest wanes. The day-to-day operations do not interest me unless there is always a new challenge.

For years I thought this was a massive weakness. More than once, I was reminded of the Turkish saying: 'Türk gibi başla, Alman gibi devam ettir, İngiliz gibi bitir', which means 'Start like a Turk, carry on like a German, and finish it like a Brit'.

My mum is English, my dad is Turkish and I spent eight of my formative years in Germany. In theory I was exposed to enough of each culture to have ended up a perfectly rounded human being. However, over the years I came to realise that I'm definitely more of a 'starter'. The passion, excitement and drive I feel when embarking on a new project, or helping other people on theirs, is one of my absolute superpowers.

When someone tells me about a business idea and it captures my imagination, I often find myself having to make a conscious effort to curb my enthusiasm.

To me, having a seed of an idea and bringing it to life is incredibly exciting. I am now fully aware that the thought of taking that first step to making an idea happen is paralysingly scary for some. That same person would, however, love the idea of taking on an existing business or project and keeping it running.

Have you got any 'weaknesses' that have been pointed out to you? Can you turn them around and adopt them as one of your superpowers?

Just because you're good at it, doesn't mean you enjoy doing it... and should be doing *more* of it.

In Part 2 we talked about how you may have ended up in a career that isn't right for you. One of the reasons for this may be that you showed promise in certain skills which you and other people may have identified. You then pursued them, somewhat blinded to the fact that you were indeed good, but you definitely didn't enjoy using said skills.

This happens more often than you might think, and if this rings true for you, you're certainly not alone. One of my clients knew he was good at client pitches. He knew this because he instinctively felt the room's full attention when he started speaking. Also, more often than not, his company was awarded the work.

Yet, whenever he finished a pitch, no matter how successful it had been, he felt completely drained of energy. He didn't enjoy performing the pitch and dreaded each one he did. Having identified the fact that he didn't enjoy doing the pitches, he immediately found a way to delegate them to someone else in the business who was not only good at pitching, but also revelled in the experience.

It takes strength to let go of your strengths.

You just haven't experienced it yet

If you feel like you just haven't found your vocation yet, I'd like to put forward the case that you haven't been exposed to the thing that is just right for you.

When I was very young, my dad used to paint a lot. He's a really skilled artist. As his work as a hotel manager started to take up more and more of his time and he was often on duty 24 hours a day, his artistic talent lay dormant for many years, until he was semi-retired.

In his mid-60s, he attended a local, government-sponsored class and tried out pottery for the first time in his life. There are few things he'd rather talk about now. He's endlessly intrigued by how to create unique patterns, how to use raw materials in unexpected ways, and how to best photograph his work to show it in its best light on Instagram.

At the age of 72, he took part in his first exhibition, and was amazed at the level of interest in his work. Not only were people interested in his work, but they loved it and bought it... by the truckload. Is there anything more exciting, more life-affirming than spending your time creating something you love, and gives others joy too?

Being the 'career nerd' I am, I asked him whether he wished he could have made a living from pottery. The answer was a resounding and emphatic "YES".

Many years ago, my friend Paul told me that he always thought he was a really bad dancer and would avoid the dancefloor at all costs. But one day, in his late teens, he was exposed to hip hop, and to his surprise realised he was a really good hip hop dancer. It was instinctive and he didn't have to try hard at all. Incidentally, he hasn't gone on to become a famous dancer, but he does feel like less of a goof on the dancefloor now.

What have you not been exposed to yet, that will turn out to be something that feeds your soul? That will feel instinctive, easy and fun?

If you've always fancied exploring an interest in more depth, right now would be a great time to do just that. Find an evening course or weekend workshop to explore and try out a new interest, or something completely random that sounds like it might be good fun.

You won't be the first person to turn a newfound hobby into a career. At worst you'll add a new string to your bow, which will contribute to your 'unique blend'. There's also a very good chance you'll become a slightly happier and certainly more interesting person.

A story cited so often that you may well be familiar with is that of a young Steve Jobs attending a calligraphy course at Reed College. That single course led him to introducing the idea of fonts when he was designing the first Macintosh computer some 10 years later. "It was the first computer with beautiful typography," Jobs said. "If I had never dropped in on that single course in college, the Mac would have never had multiple typefaces or proportionally spaced fonts."

Meet David

For 45 years, David's talents were quite literally hiding under a rock. By his own admission, he'd been a "perfectly adequate administrator" in the print business for 26 years. However, he'd been feeling dissatisfied with his job for a while. He recalls skipping across the car park when he found out that he, along with some of the other middle managers, was being made redundant. "It was one of the happiest days of my life."

He'd already spent a lot of time thinking about other work options while he was employed, but still wasn't sure what he wanted to do next. One of his options, post-redundancy, was a job in London, which would have meant a long commute. With two young daughters, he didn't fancy "shlepping" there every day.

He knew he wanted a complete lifestyle change. He also knew he enjoyed the craft side of the printing business (rather than sitting behind a desk for eight hours a day); getting out and about meeting clients and suppliers; and he knew he wanted to be outdoors as much as possible.

Stepping away from work allowed him to try out new things. Through a conversation with a friend, he found out that he was eligible for a free dry stone walling course. He signed up to do two days a week for two months, with an exam at the end of it. He absolutely took to it like a duck to water, and it further reinforced that he liked being outdoors.

When his wife signed him up for a stone carving course, he discovered that he had the uncanny ability to turn a block of stone into a beautiful piece of art, surprising himself and everyone else.

David is now an extremely content dry stone waller, who also runs stone carving courses from his home a few weekends a year.

"Stone is my thing... if I won the lottery I'd still want to go out and build stone walls (maybe not in the winter!)".

Not long after I interviewed David for my podcast, I bumped into him and his lovely wife Kaye in a cafe. He told me how the day before we met he'd been working on a wall, had taken a five-minute break, and while sipping a cup of coffee with his dog beside him, he'd enjoyed some rare March sunshine on his face and watched a buzzard soaring above him. He grinned as he told me he's never felt happier in his work. THIS, ladies and gentlemen, is the power of finding work that feeds your soul!

PART 4
Design

"The only way to do great work is to LOVE what you do"

STEVE JOBS

Finding a career that will make your heart sing is not an exact science, nor a one-size-fits-all. As we're all individuals with a completely unique set of experiences, desires and beliefs, we all have to find our individual path to uncovering our dream career. It's also worth noting that finding the next thing that's going to earn you money in a fun and meaningful way may just be a stepping stone to the next thing, and perhaps the next thing after that. It's not a single destination. Rather it's a journey that should be full of wonderful discoveries and awe-inspiring experiences – each one teaching you something new and amazing about yourself.

Defining success

'Success' is a nice word, isn't it? Most people have positive associations with it, and that may be partly because we all associate different things with the word.

More often than not, it's shaped by our experiences, our beliefs, and sometimes by what other people (hello parents!) have instilled in us.

I have worked with many people who have chased a definition of 'success' for most of their lives, only to realise that they were chasing something that ultimately didn't feel right for them.

Sometimes we get caught up following in someone else's footsteps, trying to emulate their success. There are two dangers here. One is that what they've achieved may look shiny and exciting from the outside, but may not actually be that suited to you and the lifestyle you desire. You may, for example, know people who have achieved unprecedented levels of 'success', who have completely forgotten how to laugh and enjoy themselves, and frankly take themselves far too seriously.

Secondly, trying to follow someone else's recipe for success when you don't have access to the same ingredients is an excellent way to ensure you'll ultimately meet with disappointment.

What does success mean to you? How has its meaning changed for you from five, 10, 20, 30 years ago?

In my experience, the definition of success is something that can change, sometimes drastically, throughout our lives. Our definition should evolve

– because we evolve. Our situation changes over time. Our priorities shift. What we deem highly important in our 20s may seem much less significant when we reach our 40s and 50s. What seemed incredibly important to us 10 years ago might not matter to us one bit now.

Generally speaking, we start our careers very much focused on our basic and extrinsic needs, such as buying a house, the car we've always dreamed of, the designer handbag.

As we mature and our basic extrinsic needs are met, many of us start to focus on fulfilling intrinsic needs. We come to the realisation our loved ones won't live forever; we won't live forever; and so we start looking for meaning in what we do. We seek out careers that have a more positive contribution to our community and the world at large.

Obviously this is a massive generalisation and won't ring true for everyone.

Over the years I have asked hundreds of people what success means to them, and the answers are genuinely fascinating. I have yet to hear two people give me the same answer. Our definition of success, it seems, is as unique as we are. And isn't that fabulous!? Wouldn't the world be incredibly boring if we were all striving for the same things?

Here are some of my favourite answers over the years:

- "Success means being able to do what I did today again tomorrow, and the day after that, and the day after that."
- "Just being able to hang out with my kids whenever I/they want to."
- "Owning the house of my dreams."
- "Making a positive impact on the world around me, that's all."

- "Helping real people solve real problems."
- "Finally starting to feel comfortable in myself. Not always being under pressure to be somebody else."
- "Being happy and doing something lasting and meaningful in the world."
- "To reward the people who backed me."
- "Success for me means absolutely going full tilt, making it happen, going on every adventure that I want to go on, pushing as hard as I can to make all the projects happen that I want to happen, and not leaving anything left in the tank."

But forget about everyone else's definition of what success means to them. What does it mean to you? If you really stop to think about it, what are the key indicators that you are 'successful'? It's worth taking the time to really define what success actually means to you.

Here are some exploratory questions that you can ask yourself:

- Whose definition of success have you adopted?
- Who are three people who have the most influence over you? Your thoughts, your beliefs, your actions?
- What is *their* definition of success?
- What does success mean to *you*? What does it look and feel like?

In *The Happiness Advantage*, Shawn Achor discusses the concept that happiness is at the core of success. Contrary to the common belief that success brings happiness, he argues that it is actually happiness that fosters success.

Career mission statement

Your career mission statement is basically a few sentences, or even just a few words, that mean something to you, and act as a guiding force when making decisions around your career. Its main purpose is to keep you focused whenever you're considering new job opportunities. It's a filter that you can run each opportunity through. It doesn't have to be fancy; it just needs to be meaningful to you.

My career mission statement is very simple; just like me.

I want to be doing work that is challenging, fun, rewarding and affords me the freedom to work where I want, when I want.

If it's not ticking all four boxes, I'm not interested. Obviously it's hard to know sometimes whether something will tick all the boxes until you're entrenched in the work, so you have to use your best guess.

Here are some examples of other career mission statements:

- To do work that makes a positive impact on the environment and ensures my family is always provided for.
- To pursue a career that ensures I'm always learning and contributing.
- To earn so much money that I can buy my wife and children whatever they need and desire.
- To be an inspiring leader who sees and encourages the best in people.

- To use my gift as a speaker to help and inspire people around the world.
- To use my storytelling skills to educate and entertain people.

Try this

What will your mission statement be? How can you ensure it's ingrained and top of mind?

Some people go for the simple yet effective option of writing it on a post-it note and sticking it somewhere they'll see it all the time. Others have it as their screen saver. One of my clients joked about having it tattooed on his arm. At least I think he was joking!

Your job description

There's a good chance that you have read several hundred job descriptions in your lifetime. Have you ever written a job description? Ever written one for yourself? Most people haven't. Most people have never taken the time to think deeply about how they want to spend their days.

You, however, are not 'most people'.

You are different, because writing your own job description is exactly what you are about to do.

When applying for jobs, we do our best to match our experience, education and skills to what the job description tells us the job requires. What if we were to turn this on its head? What if we start with all the skills, talents and activities we'd love to be using in our work? And only *then* match it to jobs that are undoubtedly out there, just waiting for you to come along with all your brilliance.

Sound daunting and a tad unrealistic? Good! This is where growth happens; when we step out of the norm and challenge our thinking. Trust the process! What have you got to lose?

Please believe me when I say that designing your dream job can be *extremely* fun. Think of yourself as the architect of your career. Imagine you're starting with a completely blank canvas.

> "If you can dream it, you can do it."
>
> WALT DISNEY

Have you ever been reprimanded for daydreaming? When's the last time you allowed yourself to just sit and daydream? It's a pleasure most of us deprive ourselves of, often because we don't have the luxury of time to do so, and sometimes because we consider daydreaming a complete waste of time. We live in a world where many people value productivity and efficiency over almost everything else.

Yet daydreaming is exactly what I will encourage you to do now. If you're someone who is extremely busy, I implore you to take the time to sit and do absolutely nothing and let your mind wander. The Italians have a wonderful saying for this – 'dolce far niente' – the joy of doing nothing. Somehow many of us have fallen into the trap of believing that idleness is a bad thing. But if you are normally running around like a headless chicken, then perhaps a bit of idleness would do you the world of good right now.

Here are some questions to ask yourself, sit with and then write down answers for:

- If a miracle happened while you were sleeping, and you woke up to your dream life, what would it look like?
- How many hours a week would you like to spend working ideally (bearing in mind that you will be loving your work)?
- What are the activities you are spending your days doing that are completely energising?
- What kind of people do you want to be surrounded by? Are they inspiring, clever, young, older, fun to be around? Or would you prefer to spend your days in quiet solitude? Perhaps people aren't your thing, and you just want to be around cute puppies all day.

- What kind of environment would you like to spend the majority of your time in? Do you prefer to be out in nature, or love being in an office? Do you want to be in the corner office overlooking the city, or would you prefer to be in a beautiful converted barn in the countryside?
- What impact do you want to be making on the world?
- How much will you be earning?
- What would you spend your days doing if you suddenly had £10 million in the bank?
- If you could design your perfect workday, what would it look like?
- What would an exceptional career/job look like to you?
- What would your typical day look like?
- What gives you an immense sense of satisfaction?
- Finish this sentence with as many endings as you can think of: It would be so cool if I could earn money doing...

So what will you dream up for yourself? What will you manifest? What will you believe is possible?

If you are able to identify a real need within your existing organisation for the role you've just dreamed up, an obvious and low-risk option would be to present it to your current manager. Is there an opportunity to morph your current role into one that ticks a lot more of the boxes on your new and improved job description?

Most managers don't love it when you talk only about yourself: what *you* love and what *you* would like to spend your days doing. They much prefer it when someone solves problems for them, ideally without being asked to. When someone identifies gaps, and comes up with great plans of how to plug them. When someone works out a fantastic way to save, or even better, make more money. I say *most* managers because I'm well aware of the fact that a lot of managers love the status quo, burying their heads in the sand, and getting paid to simply show up for work. If you work for someone like this, it's time for more drastic action.

If you know that your time in your current organisation is limited, you can use your dream job description as a benchmark for your job search. How? Let me give you an example.

When we lived in Sydney and I was in the early stages of building my marketing consultancy, I was looking for short-term ways to supplement my income. At the time I loved nothing more than spending hours looking at properties on real estate websites – many of which I'd never have been able to afford at the time.

So when I completed the sentence I asked you to complete just now, it went something along the lines of, "It would be so cool if I could earn money spending my days looking at awesome properties around Sydney while meeting interesting people from all around the world and using my language skills."

The obvious answer may have been to get a job as a real estate agent, but I didn't want to work weekends, so I explored other options. I stumbled across relocation companies, who help execs find homes in Sydney. I applied to become a relocation agent, and a few days later I was driving my first couple around the city, showing them properties, all the while pointing out my favourite spots in each neighbourhood we visited. Not only did I get to snoop around elegant properties, but I also met some wonderful people, some of whom I'm still friends with today.

Meet Shane

Shane's dream since the age of 12 was to become a professional rugby player. His determination, focus and discipline helped him achieve just that. As is the case with most professional athletes however, it was time for him to 'retire' from rugby before he was even 30.

As his whole world had revolved around rugby up until that time, he really had no idea what he wanted to do beyond his retirement. Through his brother, he discovered podcasts – before they were as prevalent as they are today. He encouraged his dad to create a podcast for a community project he was involved with, but when they talked through all the equipment and set-up that would be required to do so, his dad decided it was too much of a barrier. Spurred on by this problem, Shane went about creating an app which would allow people to record, share and interact via audio easily, without the need for lots of equipment and expertise. He calls this practice 'social audio'. His app, Limor, has now had more than 250,000 installs, and the business has become his main source of income.

The right environment

Imagine planting a seed in soil that contains zero nutrition, and then not watering or allowing it to see any daylight. Even though the seed may show signs of sprouting initially, it will eventually shrivel up and become one with the good-for-nothing soil.

Place the same seed in fertile soil, give it lots of attention, sunlight and water, and watch it grow and flourish into something rather beautiful.

It's the same with people. If we're in an environment where we're surrounded by the 'right people', where we're trusted, supported and lovingly encouraged, we flourish. Whether we realise it or not, camaraderie and human energy can have a massive effect on how we feel about the work we do.

The right environment can be a wonderful source of inspiration and validation. Yet the opposite can lead us to feeling frustrated, overworked and undervalued.

A client described leaving her job of 23 years to join a new organisation as "being able to breathe again". She hadn't appreciated just how much her old company had stifled her creativity, her growth and her belief in herself. She told me, "I feel like I've been on autopilot for the last two decades, and now for the first time in a very long while I truly feel like I can be me again. I really like this version of me," she added shyly.

My friend, Heather, is super passionate about her work as an HR manager. A few years ago, she found herself working in a company where her work was hugely under-appreciated. Despite being incredibly dedicated to her work and putting herself forward for several promotions, she was overlooked again and again. Over time it made her question her ability to the point where she started to doubt whether she was even in the right career.

There was only one way to find out, and that was to get a job with a different company. To her delight, she was offered a job within a few short weeks. From day one she felt like a welcome member of the team. Suddenly she was taken seriously, people wanted to hear what she had to say, and her ideas started to get implemented straight away. It's no overstatement to say she went from loathing to absolutely loving her job.

That's the power of being in the right environment!

Being surrounded by people who share your enthusiasm, your values, your passion and your interests creates a buzz and can foster a deep sense of belonging. It can also be a breeding ground for awesome ideas and positive change. The term 'Collective Effervescence' was first coined by French sociologist Emile Durkheim more than 100 years ago, and refers to the shared feeling of energy and harmony we get when we are engaged with a group of people who share our purpose. It turns out that sharing the highs and the lows, feeding off each other's energy, and even laughing together has a tremendous effect on how we feel about our work.

What environment do you want to spend your days in? What does it look and feel like?

Stop spending time on job search platforms... for now

I know from experience that spending time on job search platforms can be less fun than sticking needles in your eyes – not that I've tried sticking needles in my eyes, but I can't imagine it would be much fun.

There's a desperate hope that stumbling across a job that *sounds* exciting will provide us with the vision for our wonderful future career prospect, conveniently cutting out the need to spend precious time really getting to know yourself and *then* finding a job that will light you up. I'm sorry to say that while it's the option that may seem most obvious, it's also the least likely to yield a great outcome for you.

I wish someone had given me this advice years ago, as it would have saved me several hundred hours of depressing searching and dead-end applications. I'm told searching for love on dating apps is similarly painful, but I have no words of wisdom to impart on this topic.

If you're close to writing, or indeed handing in, your resignation letter, there's a good chance you've already spent hours, if not days, trawling unsuccessfully through countless jobs on job search platforms. Perhaps you've even applied for a few jobs already. Please stop trawling. For now. Until you've worked out exactly what you want your career to look like. Please don't jump out of the frying pan into the fire.

Refuse to choose: Becoming a multi-hyphenate

If you really want to bedazzle people, tell them you intend to become a 'multi-hyphenate'. Honestly, I didn't know what the word meant until very recently. In case you're not familiar with the term either, simply put, a multi-hyphenate is someone who has several professions. It's another way of describing someone who has a 'portfolio career'.

Many of us were brought up to believe that we should focus on one profession. One source of work and income, from one employer at a time. That works really well for some. For others, it's restrictive and not nearly stimulating enough.

Why limit yourself to a single profession or job when you have a plethora of skills, talents and interests that you want to explore and put to good use?

When I was in my 20s and just starting out in my career, the late Barbara Sher's book *Refuse To Choose* opened my eyes to the idea that you don't have to stick to a single profession. What a revelation! She calls people who can – and do – choose to engage in several professions 'scanners'. If you have many interests and can't bear to choose between them any longer, then maybe becoming a multi-hyphenate is your calling.

Limiting yourself to one job in one organisation also means you may be limiting your earning potential. Interestingly, according to the US Internal Revenue Service, millionaires earn money from an average of seven different sources. These obviously also include things like dividend income, interest on savings, rental income etc. Being a multi-hyphenate does open the opportunity to make more money from different sources and reduces the risk of being left without an income in the event of being laid off.

We are surrounded by multi-hyphenates. Here are some you may have heard of:

- Reese Witherspoon: Actor, producer, advocate, entrepreneur.
- Paris Hilton: CEO, entrepreneur, artist, DJ, model, actress, singer, humanitarian, activist, artist, investor, boss babe (her words, not mine).
- Benjamin Franklin: Politician, author, publisher, printer, scientist, inventor, statesman, diplomat, political philosopher.
- Mary Portas: Author, retail consultant, broadcaster.
- Sumiko Iwamuro aka DJ Sumirock: Dumpling restaurant proprietor by day, DJ in Tokyo clubs by night (aged in her 70s).

Meet Nigel

Nigel moved his family from the UK to Australia to become CEO of an advertising agency. When he lost his job just 11 months later, he took the slightly unconventional decision of going against everyone's well-intentioned advice to "get back on the bus" and instead took a year off.

He had no real plan other than to spend more time with his wife and kids – and lose some weight. What he didn't realise at the time was that his decision to take time out would result in him writing the highly entertaining book Fat, Forty and Fired, deliver a Ted Talk that has been watched more than 5 million times, and become a world-renowned expert on 'work-life balance'. When we caught up two decades after his unorthodox decision, he had established himself very nicely as a successful podcast host, author and professional speaker – and couldn't be happier.

PART 5
It's all in your mind

If you've ever heard of the 'Elephant Rope' story, you'll know about the elephant trainer who explains that baby elephants are tied up with a small rope which they could easily break away from as they get older. However, even when they're older they believe the rope can still hold them, so they never try to break free.

Don't be an elephant! Don't be constrained by what you think is realistic, sensible or possible!

It's okay to think outside of the box.

People are making money now in ways that we couldn't have dreamed of a few years ago. Here are some examples of some of the extraordinary ways people are earning a living:

- Trevor Hooton is a professional cuddler, charging £75/hr at the time of writing this.
- Freddie Beckitt earns a living queuing for people who are too busy or just don't enjoy queuing.
- Grace Page runs a business that enables people and businesses to book a mermaid for parties, events and filming.

I would argue strongly that your chance of finding any of these jobs by scrolling through job ads is minimal at best. With that in mind, is it possible that your dream job hasn't been created or dreamed up yet? Is it waiting for you to do so?

If it doesn't exist, create it.

Regret-proofing

It seems an obvious, almost trite, thing to say that we should spend our days focused on what's really important to us. Yet few of us do.

Palliative care nurse Bronnie Ware started a blog in 2009 which led to the best-selling book *The Top Five Regrets of the Dying*. Having spent several years in the company of those who didn't have long to live, she received a unique insight into the regrets the vast majority of us (yes, you and me included!) will experience towards the end of our lives. The most common regret she encountered was that people hadn't had the courage to live a life true to themselves, and had just done what others expected of them.

If you knew you had only three years left to live, how would you choose to spend your days? It would bring everything into sharp focus, wouldn't it?

What would you like people to say about you at your funeral? What do you want to be remembered for? What legacy do you want to leave? What impact do you want to make on the world?

When you're lying on your deathbed, will you regret not pursuing the career you always dreamed about but never had the courage to go after? Which direction will you be happy you took?

Step out of your comfort zone

Have you been sitting too comfortably for too long? Sometimes we have to fight our natural instinct in the pursuit of greater things.

Arguably, quitting your job is an extreme version of stepping out of your comfort zone.

If you're not quite ready to write your resignation letter, a really useful thing to do is experiment with other ways of stepping outside your comfort zone. Expose yourself to something you're fearful of.

Growth happens when we push ourselves to experience new things; to try things we've not done before. If we're too afraid to fail, we become too afraid to try.

It's entirely possible that trying out something that feels uncomfortable will lead to one or more of the following:

- Clarity on your current work situation.
- Newfound appreciation for your work.
- Confidence boost.
- New ideas.
- Fresh perspective.
- Reminder that you're capable of so much more than you realise.
- Courage to quit your job.

Try this

Three things I can do that are out of the ordinary for me are:

1.
2.
3.

Meet Koj

Andrew Kojima (affectionately known as Koj) left university aged 22 and, attracted by the big bright lights of London, went straight onto 'the treadmill' and into the world of investment banking. Thinking back to these early days now, he recalls, "I felt that I'd fallen into finance rather than actively chosen it."

When he and his wife started looking at moving out of London, he considered leaving his finance job and working as a consultant, but his heart wasn't in it. At a crossroads and trying to work out where to take his career, he said, "I literally made a list of things I wanted to do."

One passion he'd always had was cooking, and when he started to experience what he refers to as a "mini, early midlife crisis", he decided to step out of his comfort zone and take the brave move of giving MasterChef a go. At the time he felt like it was somewhat unachievable and out of his control because the year he applied, there'd been more than 24,000 applicants. He not only managed to get onto the show, he also became a finalist.

Becoming a finalist on MasterChef provided him with a springboard to open his own restaurant, become a published author, run pop-up dinners and cook for the rich and famous – among other things.

Meet Sally

Sally was an accountant for more than 20 years. She was good at her job but even just the thought of work filled her with dread. After two decades, she realised there was not a single thing she enjoyed about her job anymore. She was ready for a change. What's more, she knew exactly what she wanted to do. She wanted to be a full-time artist. Financially, she was quite comfortable because she had plenty of savings and her husband was happy to support the family for up to a year.

The only thing holding Sally back was the paralysing fear of putting her work out there and being judged by it. When we talked about her fear, she likened it to those awful dreams where you're standing in front of a crowd completely naked. The thought of having her artwork on display for sale made her feel exposed and vulnerable. When we explored her fear, we uncovered the fact that while she was scared of selling her work, just having it exhibited somewhere was "totally fine". You may have already guessed what happened next. I gently encouraged her to join an exhibition which showcased local artists' work. It was a little bit out of her comfort zone, but not enough for her to find a million reasons not to do it.

The exhibition changed her life. Far from feeling exposed, she relished the opportunity to chat to people about her work and felt immense pride with every compliment she received. Even more exciting was the fact that several people asked if her work was for sale. She found herself agreeing to sell several pieces in one evening. Fast forward three years and Sally has left her accountancy job and is fulfilling commissions.

The luck factor

"Luck is where preparation meets opportunity."

SENECA

I used to be slightly envious of people who appeared to have been born knowing exactly what they were meant to do in life. Those who just always knew they wanted to be a doctor, for example, had the right amount of intelligence, access to education, and the perfect temperament to become an absolutely fantastic doctor. They never question whether they're in the right job. They just know they are, and are blissfully fulfilling what was meant to be. If you spend any time with these people, they'll often say that they "feel very lucky".

This reference to luck isn't reserved for those who knew from an early age what they wanted to do. What is fascinating is that the belief that they're lucky is something that unites them with those who have found work that they love in later life, through an often much more lengthy process of exploration. Pretty much everyone I've interviewed for my podcast to date has claimed they were lucky at some point – completely unprompted by me. Incidentally, people who love their work also almost always have an optimistic view on life. They are confident in themselves and their abilities, and they have a huge amount of determination.

But what about the rest of us mere mortals? Those of us who believe we are less lucky? Or worse, never have any luck at all. In fact, we're the most unlucky people alive. Nothing good ever happens to us. We are never presented with any good opportunities. We never get the promotion, or get asked to be involved in the juicy projects at work.

If words like luck, optimism, confidence and perseverance are alien to you or simply don't feature very heavily in your vocabulary, then there's every chance you'll find it difficult to extract yourself from a job that's making you miserable. Your lack of faith in things turning out just how you hope they might is very likely to keep you exactly where you are now.

Luckily, your luck is about to turn. It's about to turn – very simply – because of your decision to make it turn.

Richard Wiseman, wrote a wonderful book called *The Luck Factor*. His extensive research into what makes some people luckier than others is hugely insightful. One of the main findings is so simple it's almost comical. The main thing that lucky people have in common is simply that they expect to be lucky, which means you can decide right now that you too are lucky. You can decide that even when things don't work out as you expected, you're lucky because it will ultimately lead you to something even better than you could have imagined.

On top of that, you can start putting yourself in situations that drastically increase your chances of being lucky.

So much of your luck depends on you just showing up. Going on that course. Attending that networking event. Speaking to that stranger in the post office queue. Picking up the phone to someone you haven't spoken to for a long time. Sending that email. In short, it boils down to taking more chances and being open to the fact that you're going to get lucky.

Sometimes it really is just about being in the right place at the right time. But believing that's all there is to it renders us somewhat powerless.

How much more control would you have over your life if you actively created possibilities and opportunities?

> *"The more I practise, the luckier I get."*
>
> GARY PLAYER

A few years ago when I was in a job that I quite enjoyed, I couldn't shake the feeling that I was meant to be doing something else. I knew I had skills and things that I really enjoyed doing that I just wasn't able to put to use in the job I was in. I had a clear list of things I wanted out of my next job. The kind of people I'd be spending my time with, the kind of environment I'd be in, the kind of events I'd be organising, the hours I'd be working, the salary I'd be paid. The only thing I wasn't clear on was what the actual job would be. In fact I really had no idea. I certainly hadn't come across a job that encapsulated everything I dreamed of. However, having created a clear picture in my head of the details, on a whim, I checked a job search platform. The first job that came up made my heart race. The job description pretty much matched the job description I'd created for myself. My luck didn't end there.

At the time I was a committee member of a local organisation. The same week I came across my 'dream job', I overheard the chairperson of the committee talking to someone about the role I now felt I was destined for. I politely butted in and he told me a friend of his had close links to the organisation that was advertising my dream job. I asked for an introduction and the gentleman in question was kind enough to fill me in on some of the back story. To cut a long story short, I got an interview and was offered the job. I'll never know whether I would have been in with a chance without knowing some of the background, but I definitely felt 'lucky' to have had that rather fortunate encounter.

Try this

Every day for the next week, start a sentence with "I was so lucky today..." when you're speaking to someone.

Examples

- "I was so lucky… I got to the petrol station and I managed to get a pump without having to queue like normal."
- "I was so lucky today… I got the last Danish pastry in the bakery."
- "I was so lucky today… I sat next to a super interesting guy on the train to work."
- "I was so lucky today… a friend offered me a ticket to see my favourite band."
- "I was so lucky today… I bought a winning lottery ticket!"

What are you paying attention to?

Your brain isn't able to take in and process every single piece of information it is exposed to, so it focuses on what it considers the most important, most relevant, most likely to keep you safe.

The cool thing is that you get to choose what you put your focus on. If you fancy focusing on all the doom and gloom out there, go right ahead. Knock yourself out! You'll find a million reasons why you should never do anything, least of all quit a job that's no longer serving you.

If we're looking for evidence that you should never take any risks you don't have to look far at all. There are wars, people dying of hunger, global viruses, economic instability, corruption. I mean I could go on for hours. *Or* you can choose to focus your attention on things that support a more positive view of the world. For every corrupt politician there are thousands of really decent people who wake up every day wanting to 'do the right thing'. For every natural disaster that catches the media's attention, there are a hundred good news stories that don't necessarily make the headlines.

We're not designed to know what's going on in every corner of the world all the time. A hundred years ago, if there was an earthquake that tragically killed thousands of people on the other side of the world, there's a good chance you'd never hear about it. Yet today, traditional news outlets will stream hours of footage, detailing every heart-breaking moment of the disaster. Interviews with people who have lost loved ones, who have lost their homes, who are still stuck under the wreckage. It's devastating and incredibly distressing to watch.

I'm not saying we should bury our heads in the sand or be unsympathetic, but surely focusing on things that you can actually affect or that serve you is the much more intelligent way to go about life.

> *"God, grant me the serenity to accept the things I cannot change, the courage to change the things I can, and the wisdom to know the difference."*
>
> Reinhold Neibuhr

If you're serious about taking your career in a new and exciting direction, find things to read and listen to that inspire you, that make you laugh, that give you practical insight into the kind of work you'd love to do. Never before in history have we had such easy access to so much incredible content. You can listen to interviews with inspiring people all day, every day if you so wish. You're just a few clicks away from finding out about pretty much anything that interests you.

Choose what you pay attention to wisely. Use it as an enabler, not yet another excuse not to take action.

What's coming out of your mouth?

Have you ever noticed how infectious, interesting and attractive it is when someone talks about something with genuine passion? It's hard not to get caught up in their excitement and enthusiasm. Imagine I told you that I'm now going to talk to you for several hours about the growth, movement, reproduction and survival of plants. While I know that sounds super exciting for a small proportion of the population, I would wager a guess that to most people this sounds like the perfect topic to fall asleep to.

However, if I tell you that it's in fact David Attenborough who will be doing the storytelling, you may be more interested and willing to stay awake. That's because he is so passionate about the topics he speaks on, that it's nigh on impossible not to get caught up in his enthusiasm.

Conversely, I'm sure we've all come across our fair share of 'negatrons'. People who drain us of energy. They may be perfectly well-intentioned people who don't even realise they're doing it, but they seem to enjoy spreading their misery and negativity. Given half the chance they will tell you in graphic detail about all the things that are going wrong in their lives. All the people that are making their life a misery. All the things they hate about their job. All the reasons they couldn't possibly leave.

They're perpetually focused on the negative. Their boss hates them. They hate their boss. They're not being paid nearly enough money. They're overqualified for their dead-end role. The list goes on.

As you can probably imagine, I find it very hard to listen to people moan and complain about their work. In my late 20s I had a job that I really loved. I worked as a business adviser for a not-for-profit organisation in Sydney. It was great fun because I got to meet and work with a huge variety of small business owners and (hopefully) have a positive impact on them. What was much less fun was the office environment. For some reason there was a culture of whining about things – everything – constantly. As I've always been a good, empathetic listener, I often found myself being on the receiving end of the constant barrage of negativity. *They* would go away from their little whinge feeling lighter, having had someone listen to them, and *I* was left feeling a tonne heavier.

By the end of each working day, I would come home exhausted and unable to focus on all the positive, exciting conversations I'd had with clients throughout the day. I was one of the more junior members of staff, so I felt like I didn't have the jurisdiction to make a significant change in this complaining culture. One day, after a particularly whingey, draining conversation I decided enough was enough. I grabbed a piece of A4 paper and wrote "1 whinge = $1". That is, if you're going to come and spew a load of negativity at me, that's fine as long as you pay me $1. I stuck it on the wall by my head. Miraculously the complaining (at least to me) ceased immediately.

Are you a positron or negatron? This is possibly going to be a bit confronting for you, but I want you to be really honest with yourself about which one you are. Are you someone who talks with delight about their work? Or do you make people want to stab themselves in the eyes with something really hot rather than listen to you moan about it?

If you feel there might be a slight chance you've fallen into the habit of being a negatron, I'm sorry to be the bearer of bad news; you are not making any friends complaining about your work and how miserable it's making you. Or maybe you *are* making friends as a result of whinging. You've found someone to enjoy a cosy little doom loop with. They will likely revel in your negativity marathon and do their very best to ensure you stay in your perpetual state of unhappiness. Just know that there are no winners in this race.

Before I lose you completely, please know that extracting yourself from this perpetual cycle of gloom is something you have complete control over, and you can implement and see results from it immediately. Ready for a fun experiment? From now on don't say *anything* negative about your work – to anyone! Not your best friend, your mum, your colleague, the guy serving you coffee, your neighbour or your long-suffering spouse. No one!

If you find yourself wanting to have a whinge or a moan, just zip up those lips and don't say anything. If you really have to get it out of your system, write it down, then tear it up or burn it. Remember your mum's advice: "If you can't say anything nice, don't say anything at all"? This is the adult, work-related version of her well-meaning – and sage – advice.

If you're someone who is unhappy in your work but aren't vocal about it, congratulations! You may skip the step above. Here's a little something for you to try out instead. When next asked how your job is going, say, "It's going quite well actually. This week I really had fun doing..." (insert all the things you noticed you enjoyed, even if it's just one tiny thing).

Become hyper-aware of what's coming out of your mouth. You might find that you rather enjoy talking about positive stuff. For bonus points, notice how people respond to you. You may find that people don't immediately glaze over and excuse themselves. They might even stick around and ask to hear more.

Positivity can be your secret weapon, and approaching any changes in your career with this weapon will make all the difference.

Mindfulness

"Change your thoughts and change your world."

NORMAN VINCENT PEALE

What's your process for making good decisions? Do you make a list and weigh up all the pros and cons? Do you have a mentor to talk things through with? Do you toss a coin? Do you go with your gut instinct?

Making big life decisions can be really challenging, especially when many of us are already suffering from 'decision fatigue'. It's estimated that the average person is faced with approximately 35,000 decisions a day. That's 2000 decisions an hour! Many of which we make subconsciously.

Which TV programme should I watch? Should I bother shaving today? Which members of my team do I let go to reduce my team by 10 per cent as requested by senior management? Should I have breakfast or try fasting until lunchtime? Should I continue reading this book? (Yes, you should!)

It's no wonder then that people like Facebook founder Mark Zuckerberg, who are making decisions which are likely to impact millions of people every day, actively look for ways to reduce the amount of decisions they have to make. One of Mark's strategies for this is to limit what he wears to a simple t-shirt and jeans.

Often when people tell me they've lost touch with what makes them tick, it's because they have lost the art of listening to their instinct. Making important decisions is a whole lot easier when we're able to cut out all the noise and learn to listen to our gut. Being mindful helps us to tap into our deepest desires. Our inner knowing is pretty wise and we do better when we learn to listen to it. Have you ever gone to bed with a problem whirling around in your head, and thus kept you awake? Next time that happens, try this fun experiment. Ask your subconscious brain to give you an answer by the morning, take a deep breath, smile, trust that it will, and go to sleep. See what happens in the morning!

Meditation

If you're already a convert to the endless benefits of meditation, you may give yourself a pat on the back, skip this part altogether and jump to the next chapter. If the concept of meditation is new to you, or something you just haven't got your head around, please read on.

Contrary to popular belief, mediation doesn't have to involve sitting completely still, cross legged, under a tree somewhere in the middle of nowhere, in complete silence for hours on end. In fact I have come to associate meditation with deliciously luxurious time out for myself. Spurred on by the words of meditation master davidji – "Feather your nest, comfort is queen" – my lavender eye mask and a cosy blanket are now very much part of my meditation ritual, which is usually 10-15 mins each day.

But even if you don't feel you have 10 minutes a day to yourself, research has shown that simply focusing on your breath for two minutes a day can have quite a dramatic effect. You can do it anywhere, anytime you have two minutes to spare.

The 4-7-8 breathing exercise

1. Empty your lungs and inhale through your nose while counting to four in your head.
2. Hold your breath to the count of seven.
3. Exhale through your mouth for a count of eight.
4. Repeat this process consecutively three or four times in a row.
5. Notice how you feel afterwards.

In all honesty, I only discovered the power of meditation in earnest when I was in my early 40s. I say "in earnest" because I was exposed to it much earlier in life, but never really understood the value of it until relatively recently. In fact, I remember vividly the first time I listened to a meditation on a CD, in which Paul Mckenna led the listener through the meditation. I found it so funny I giggled all the way through it. I now wish I'd discovered the power of meditation sooner. Here are some of the reasons I'm a huge advocate for meditation and why I strongly believe it can play a big part in your career.

1. A clear head: Just a few minutes of meditation a day has been shown to improve mental clarity by eliminating the stream of jumbled thoughts that are swirling around in your mind. Who doesn't want that when you're assessing your skills, interests and values – and you're on the verge of making life-altering decisions?

2. Stress reduction: Most big life changes are inevitably accompanied by a level of stress, uncertainty and anxiety. Meditation is known to be a super effective antidote to stress. Much more effective than alcohol, sugar, smoking and a myriad of other things we tend to engage in when we feel stressed. It gently encourages our brains to focus on the here and now, rather than worrying about something that's just happened or is about to happen. The 4-7-8 breathing exercise is a quick and easy way to lower blood pressure. It takes less than two minutes and you can do it anywhere, anytime.

3. Creativity: Getting into a habit of dialling our internal dialogue down on a regular basis, can help you to start to see things in a fresh light and think more creatively.

4. Emotional regulation: Have you ever had to make decisions under pressure? While some people are actually extremely good decision-makers when under pressure, most prefer to have a calm mind when seeking a positive outcome. Making decisions in a calm state tends to lead to much better outcomes, or at the very least give a sense of control.

5. Self-awareness: Meditation provides an opportunity for self-reflection and self-discovery. It encourages you to explore your values, interests and aspirations on a deeper level. By creating a regular meditation practice, you can cultivate self-awareness and gain insights into your strengths, weaknesses and potential areas for personal growth. This self-reflection can aid you in making a career change that aligns more closely with your authentic self and long-term fulfilment.

6. Resilience and adaptability: A regular meditation practice can help cultivate resilience, which is the ability to bounce back from setbacks and embrace change. Meditation encourages a non-judgmental attitude and the acceptance of impermanence, which can contribute to a greater sense of adaptability, flexibility and inner peace.

7. Intuition: You've probably spent most of your life leading with your head. In fact you may have been making a conscious effort to ignore your heart. Now is the time to start leading more with your heart. What is your heart telling you when you really stop to listen to it? All the cues are there, we're just not always great at listening to them.

8. Confidence: Just a few minutes of regular meditation can make you feel more confident and self-assured.

While I wouldn't rely solely on a meditation practice to make good decisions about your career, it is an incredibly powerful practice that can support your decision-making process. The positive effect it will undoubtedly have on your overall wellbeing is an added bonus.

There are lots of apps to help you along the way. Here are just a few:

- Insight Timer.
- Calm.
- Headspace.
- The Healthy Minds Program.

Despite all the benefits of meditation, it's not for everyone. If you have given it a good try, and it's just not for you don't beat yourself up about it. Different strokes for different folks, folks! Maybe engaging in mindful activities is more your thing.

Mindful activities

We engage in mindful activities that we find fun and engaging all the time as kids, but when we're adults it tends to become less of a priority.

But when do you have your best ideas? When is your mind razor sharp? When does the answer to the question you've been repeatedly asking yourself suddenly pop into your head as if by magic?

Often it's when the mind is slightly disengaged, and we've lost ourselves in an enjoyable activity. This is because being engrossed in the activity tends to regulate our emotions and reduce our stress levels. It's essentially giving the brain some much needed rest and space to start coming up with positive, creative, clear thoughts. It stops all the constant internal chatter, and forces us to be in the moment. When we're completely consumed by the activity, and our worries fall away, something quite magical can happen. This in turn can lead to an epiphany and bring clarity to unresolved career issues you may have been experiencing.

Some examples of mindful activities include:

- Walking in silence, observing nature.
- Colouring in.
- Jogging.
- Surfing.
- Craft such as pottery, knitting, crocheting.
- Baking or cooking.
- Gardening.
- Woodwork.

- Sitting back and listening to your favourite music.
- Beekeeping.

Meet Martin

Beekeeping was a hobby that Martin had squeezed into his busy schedule while he had been in full-time employment. He'd had a successful career in the same industry for 27 years, but in reaching midlife, he suddenly felt compelled to try something completely new.

"I hadn't experienced anything else. I hadn't done anything else. I hadn't tried anything else. I hadn't worked in different companies and experienced different things. So I think it was like, you know what, let's see if I can turn my hand to something else". And turn his hand to something else he did!

With the support of his wife, he quit his job, not knowing what he was going to do next. It was only when he took six months off that the peace and solace he found while beekeeping gave him the 'aha' moment he was looking for. The answer had been right in front of him all along.

He decided to try and turn his passion for beekeeping into a business. He founded Knight Beekeeping, which enables organisations to have their own beehives. Martin installs, cares for, and maintains the beehives, runs 'Experience Days' and helps to harvest the honey. Two years on from taking the big leap, he's back to earning what he was earning in his full-time office job – and "loving every minute".

Manifestation

If you've only vaguely heard of the concept of manifestation and think it's something exclusively practised by the spiritually inclined, and it's definitely not for pragmatic, realistic people like you, then please stick around.

Manifestation at its core is about setting intentions. Intentions that are aligned with your values and what you truly desire. Manifestation, sometimes referred to as the 'law of attraction' helps to focus your subconscious mind, and can be really useful in helping you to believe that something you dream of could actually happen. This in turn enables you to show up differently; with more confidence, more hope, more faith, more focus, more resilience. It opens the mind up to being on the lookout for opportunities that will get you a step closer to your dream career. In other words, it will help you to get your butt and your brain into gear.

I love asking clients what they're focusing on. What are they spending the majority of their time, thoughts and energy on? It gives me – and them – a great insight into why they're feeling stuck. We get more of what we put our focus on. There's a really simple way to demonstrate this theory. Look around the room and notice everything that's yellow. Now close your eyes and recall everything that is blue. Chances are that you won't be able to remember anything blue. That's because your brain was too focused on the yellow. It's the same with career opportunities that we may miss because we're too focused on the 'wrong' things; things that aren't aligned with what we actually truly desire.

Creating a vision board

A vision board is a great visualisation tool that can help you to clarify your goals, make them appear much more real and achievable, and vastly enhance your motivation and focus. There's some great fun to be had with it.

There are different ways of creating a vision board. It can be as simple as writing a list of specific things you want to attract. Alternatively, if you want to get the creative juices flowing, you can make a collage of images that represent the things you want to invite into your life. The more specific the better. It's significant to note that the things you want to attract do need to contain an element of you being able to control the outcome. So putting a lottery win on your vision board, for example, is futile because beyond buying a lottery ticket you don't have any control over winning. On the other hand, if you wanted to work with a particular organisation, you could absolutely include that. You set the intention and your mind is then receptive to any opportunities that bring you a step closer to that goal. Some of those opportunities will be very deliberately created by you, and some will 'magically' land in your lap.

Despite the fact that I've been a big fan of vision boards for many years, their effectiveness still takes me by complete surprise sometimes.

Many of the visions I've laid out on vision boards have manifested in ways that frankly freak me out a little. For example, when I started YES Career Coaching, I had a very clear vision of the sort of people I would like as clients. There was one lady in particular who embodied all the characteristics I was hoping for in my future clients. She'd been a client of mine when I ran my marketing consultancy in Sydney more than a decade before. She was positive, hard-working, determined, friendly and executed everything we discussed diligently and with joy. I found a testimonial she'd written about me and my services at the time, printed it out and stuck it on my vision board. I shouldn't have been surprised then, that she was one of the first people who contacted me to enquire about help with their career pivot. I hadn't heard from her in more than 10 years. I hadn't expected her to contact me and become a client; I had merely been manifesting a desire to work with people *like* her. Obviously I was delighted to work with her again, and many more clients just like her followed too.

Arnold Schwarzenegger, who has famously changed careers very successfully several times, recalls how he spent hours alone at home working out in silence, all the while reflecting on how he was going to move from his boyhood home in Austria to the US, visualising becoming a bodybuilding champion, and making millions of dollars. Reportedly his mother was concerned that while other teenage boys had pictures of women on their bedroom walls, Arnold's wall was adorned with pictures of half-naked, ripped men – his idols.

If you're sceptical about whether manifestation could work for you, why not give it a try anyway? What's the worst that could happen? Best case it turns out to be an absolute game-changer and you actually get what you want. If it really doesn't work, the worst that will happen is that you've spent an afternoon having a bit of fun creating something – engaging in a mindful activity! Plus, you get the satisfaction of telling everyone you were right not to believe all this manifestation nonsense!

It would be remiss of me at this point not to stress that simply creating a vision board and then sitting around waiting for the magic to happen is most probably not going to work. The real power of manifestation lies in the action that accompanies your vision.

Confidence

I venture to suggest that confidence in yourself and your abilities will be your absolute best friend on your career journey. Such a big part of fulfilling your potential is believing in it in the first place. A lack of confidence can stem from stories we tell ourselves. Unkind things people have said to, or about, us. It can be the result of rejection, or having neglected or forgotten about all the things we're good at. Often it strikes when we least expect it, and many times when it's least convenient.

We all have certain situations and certain times when we feel more confident than in others. Being at a crossroads in our career is definitely a time that we most need a strong sense of self and oodles of confidence. So how do we go about conjuring it up when it's selfishly deserted us in our hour of need?

I've already touched on the fact that meditation can help increase your self-confidence. Here are some other things to try if you feel like an injection of confidence wouldn't go amiss.

Earn your confidence

A great way to earn confidence is to deliberately put yourself in situations that feel uncomfortable. Do things that scare you slightly. Pushing through that awkward feeling and coming out at the other end helps us to realise that what we feared hasn't in fact killed us. It merely made us stronger.

I attribute at least some of my self-confidence to the fact that when I was little my dad used to send me back to the counter when he was half-way through his McDonalds sundae, and ask for more chocolate sauce. Presumably he thought I had a better chance of not being told "no". I was mortified the first time. I felt like I was going to die of embarrassment and wanted the ground to swallow me up. Spoiler alert! I survived the ordeal... several times in fact. *And* I managed to come away with a little mountain of sauce every time.

Channelling your inner Trump

Whatever you may think of former US president Donald Trump, he does seem to have an unshakable belief in himself and his abilities. On days when you question yourself and your abilities, try channelling your 'inner Trump'. If Trump is offensive to you, choose someone else who comes across as extremely confident.

When driving across America a few years ago, I was struck by the number of "What would Jesus do?" car stickers. Regardless of your religious beliefs, the sticker is a good reminder to behave like someone else when we're out of our depth. Perhaps someone more noble, more moral, more holy, more self-assured. If you're struggling to muster the confidence to take the first step towards a career that will almost certainly bring you joy, whose energy can you channel?

Positive self-talk

How you talk to yourself is crucial in how you then feel about yourself. If you spend your days berating yourself and beating yourself up about all of your failings, it's going to be an impossible challenge to feel good about who you are. Notice how you think about yourself. Can you be mindful about noticing all your best attributes? Can you make a conscious effort to be kinder with your self-talk? Can you be deliberate about shutting down the internal voice that is pointing out your shortcomings?

I see YOU!

Who are the people who make you feel confident about yourself and what you're capable of? The ones who notice things that others have failed to see. The ones who see something special in you and, importantly, are vocal about it.

Those are the people you need in your life right now. Spend more time with them!

Having someone who not only sees your brilliance but encourages you to fulfil it can have a huge impact on your confidence and subsequently your career path. One of my clients who met a wonderful man after being in an abusive relationship for many years put it beautifully: "He helped me believe in myself again, and it was truly the first time I'd dare to believe in myself for more than a decade. Now I feel like I can conquer the world."

Conversely, who makes you feel a bit useless? Who is quick to point out your faults and undesirable traits? You may not be able to cut these people out of your life completely, but you can surely choose to spend less time with them. At the very least you can choose to smile and let their words of discouragement wash over you.

Oh, you're good at that!

Hopefully by now you've identified some things that you're above averagely good at. What activities make you feel confident? Incorporating more of those activities in your day-to-day life will have a dramatic effect on how you feel about yourself. They could be playing football, crocheting, teaching your child maths, juggling, playing chess, writing poetry, painting, doing sudoku. Anything that you're good at and enjoy doing.

Try this

1. Make a list of the things and people that make you feel confident.
2. Add to your lists whenever you discover something or someone that falls into either category.
3. Make a point of doing more of the activities and spend more time with those who give you a confidence boost.

Becoming an avid collector of your wins

We're instinctively good at keeping score of things that didn't quite go our way. Little wins pass us by because we're not focused on them. Can you start becoming an avid collector of little (and big!) wins? Collect your wins like little trinkets. Write them down somewhere. Become hyper aware of them rather than letting them slip through your consciousness unnoticed and unappreciated. On days when your confidence is low, grab your list and remind yourself of all the things that make you more than worthy of feeling good about yourself.

- A compliment from a stranger.
- Making someone's day by complimenting *them*.
- Managing to get those eight hours of sleep you promised yourself.
- Cooking up a delicious meal.
- Praise for a job well done.
- Fitting in the gym workout.
- Getting the grumpy barista to crack a smile.
- Snagging a parking space right outside the restaurant on a rainy day.
- Getting your hands on the last oven-fresh croissant at your favourite cafe.

Pride-worthy achievements

It's a rather unfortunate fact that very few of us sit around reflecting on all the things we've achieved over the years and thinking about how wonderful we are. In reality, most people tend to have a bias towards beating themselves up about all the things they haven't achieved yet, all the things they haven't succeeded at and the aspirations they're still chasing. Now is your opportunity to be unashamedly boastful, and congratulate yourself on being a rather marvellous human being. We've all done things that we can feel proud of and that are worth celebrating. The aim of reflecting on our achievements is not just to make us feel good about ourselves for a while. The main reason it's so important to take the time to do this is because it can give us wonderful insight into the kind of things we've done that are significant to us, and consequently design a career around things that are meaningful; that make us feel good about ourselves and our triumphs.

Try this

Part 1
Make a list of all the things you've achieved in your life, in and outside of work. What are you super proud of? List as many pride-worthy things you can think of, and then challenge yourself to find another five. If you're struggling to find things, ask people who know and love you to contribute.

Part 2
Give yourself a metaphorical (or if your arms will stretch that far, a real) pat on the back.

Part 3
Is there a common theme in your accomplishments? What is it?

Curiosity killed the cat

It may have killed the cat, but curiosity could be one of your best allies when it comes to your career. As annoying as it can be for the adult on the receiving end of an endless barrage of banal questions from a young child, we should really take inspiration from said child. They're asking because they're curious, and there's a very good chance that you were once a super curious, possibly slightly annoying child yourself. Over the years, that curiosity has been beaten out of us, probably by one too many adults begging us to please stop asking why the sky is blue and whether god is real.

Becoming more curious is one of the best things you can do if you're unsure of where you want your career to go. Upping your curiosity levels is a surefire way to open yourself up to exciting opportunities that you may have dismissed until now without really exploring their true potential. You never know where following your curiosity may lead you. Next time someone suggests something to you, be it a completely new career path or a change of hairstyle, can you try to receive their suggestion with curiosity instead of batting it away immediately? Ask them to elaborate on their suggestion. Ask them some open-ended questions. Stay curious and open to changing your mind about things.

PART 6
Your Body

Forming new habits

"People do not decide their futures, they decide their habits and their habits decide their futures."

F. M. ALEXANDER

We all have good and bad habits. Habits that make us healthier, happier, more productive, or conversely more overweight, less active, less content.

Are your actions in line with what you dream of? Let me ask that question another way. Are you consciously taking some kind of action every day to get you closer to your dream career?

Which of your existing habits will help you achieve your dream career? Is it time to ditch some of your existing habits and replace them with new ones?

Forming good habits will support and potentially supercharge your journey to a more fulfilling career. The first step is to identify which of your existing habits are acting as a barrier to change, and then work out what new habits are likely to serve you better.

Examples of habits that might be holding you back:

- Hanging out with the 'wrong' people. People who drain you of energy, who complain a lot, who have nothing positive or interesting to say.
- Sleeping less than seven-eight hours per night.
- Eating an excessive amount of junk food.
- Spending too much time watching or reading mainstream news.

Here are examples of habits that may serve you:

- Spending time with people who inspire and encourage you.
- Reading books, articles and news stories that fill you with awe and hope for what is possible.
- Listening to podcasts while you go for a walk in nature.
- Exercising.
- Adding one extra portion of vegetables to your meal, instead of an extra helping of carbohydrates.

Changing our habits is often much harder than we'd like and expect. Some are so deep-rooted that we're not even consciously aware of them anymore. Most of us don't wonder, for example, whether we can be bothered to brush our teeth before we go to bed. We just do it. It's a habit that's been drilled into us from a very early age, and we do it without having a daily internal debate about whether or not we should brush them today.

We develop habits through repetitive actions to the extent that they ingrain themselves into our subconscious and become encoded within the nerve cells of our brain. So it stands to reason that breaking habits that aren't serving us anymore will require a bit of conscious effort.

If you'd told me five years ago that I would become a regular gym-goer and, more importantly, enjoy going to the gym, I would have laughed at you. I genuinely couldn't think of a less fun way to exercise at the time. However, as I entered my 40s, I became aware of how important weight bearing exercise is for women in the prevention of osteoporosis, in weight management, mental wellbeing and hormonal balance, to name but a few benefits.

Going to the gym most probably would have been a complete slog for me, had it not been for the following:

The right environment: I definitely didn't want to go to a gym that was full of people who grunt their way through each exercise and stop to check themselves out in the mirror every three seconds. No thanks! Instead I found a hotel gym down the road that, thankfully, is pretty quiet most of the time. I'm often the only person there. Bliss!

The social aspect: I started my journey into becoming a regular gym-goer with a couple of close friends. We spurred each other on, and because we didn't want to let each other down we invariably stick to our weekly routine.

A positive association: I've always enjoyed exercise and have always liked playing tennis, golf, volleyball etc. Going to the gym didn't appeal to me years ago because I associated it with boring repetitions and being indoors, when I much prefer variety and being outdoors. However, by injecting my gym sessions with something I love doing (learning), I created a positive association with them. I now love the fact that I get uninterrupted time listening to a podcast while I work out. Honestly, the cocktail of listening to something super stimulating or entertaining while working out is better than any mojito I've ever tasted!

Reward: I usually reward myself with two things after the gym session. A coffee and chat with my friend *and* a swim and chillout in the pool area.

Ironically, I enjoy my workouts so much now that the coffee, chat and chillout are no longer essential but a nice little bonus. You know you've really cracked a habit when you approach it with the mindset "I WANT to" rather than "I HAVE to".

What can you do to associate change with pleasure, and make the barrier to taking the first step towards change much easier to overcome?

Your health

> *"Give me six hours to chop down a tree and I will spend the first four sharpening the axe."*
>
> ABRAHAM LINCOLN

If you are someone who looks after themselves physically, you're already in on the secret that your physical wellbeing makes all the difference to how you feel about yourself, and massively affects your decision-making ability, your energy, your confidence and, very likely, also your happiness levels. It makes you more resilient and able to cope with stressful situations. Looking after yourself and your body sends your brain the message that you matter.

Neglecting our physical health often leads to the exact opposite. It makes us feel sluggish, uninspired, riddled with self-doubt and insecurities, and unable to cope well with adversity.

Being in poor health can affect every aspect of our lives and will almost certainly cloud our judgement when it comes to the important things.

In extreme cases ailing health leads to the ultimate ultimatum. The term 'burnout' was originally coined in the 1970s by the American psychologist Herbert Freudenberger, and is now something that many of us are, sadly, all too familiar with. In my line of work, it's become a term that is mentioned far too frequently. Even if we haven't experienced it ourselves, we probably know at least one person who has experienced physical and emotional exhaustion, brought on by prolonged or repeated stress. In many cases it leads to anxiety and depression.

Mental Health UK polled 2,060 working adults in the UK and the findings in their *Burnout Report 2024* are staggering. "With nine in 10 adults in the UK experiencing high or extreme stress in the past year and one in five needing to take time off work due to poor mental health caused by pressure or stress, we must focus on challenging the causes of chronic stress across society and preventing burnout."

Meet Jim

It wasn't until Jim had a breakdown in a meeting with his boss that he realised just how much things had to change for him. He'd had a successful international career as General Counsel to companies such as Ryanair, Etihad and Uber. However, over the years he felt like he was living a 'half-life' and was constantly going to doctors complaining of a lack of energy. Each time he did, he'd come out with a clean bill of health, being told everything was fine.

When I interviewed him and his wife Natasa for my podcast, he told me that he felt like his body had been keeping score during his time in those highly stressful jobs, and that it all came to a head one day.

"I literally broke down in a couple of meetings with my boss and it scared the hell out of me that I literally couldn't function. And that was a big wake up call for me".

What ensued was a complete lifestyle overhaul. His desire to live another 50 years and spend quality time with his kids and wife gave him the impetus and drive to change habits around his health.

It wasn't long before people started to notice big changes in him. During our three-way conversation, Natasa mentioned that she used to lovingly refer to him as 'Mr Bellyman'. Now she can barely hide her pride (or take her eyes off him!) as she declares: "He's a super-strong, well-built person... he's 50 but looks much better than the majority of 25-year-olds."

When friends and family started asking how he was improving his health and performance, Jim and Natasa started setting little challenges for them. That's when they realised there was an opportunity to share all the things they'd learned on their journey, and created a whole business around it.

If you haven't reached breaking point yet, but feel like it may be on the horizon, then today – right now – is the time to start doing something about it. Don't leave it until it's too late. If you're not sure where to start and think you might need professional help from a nutritionist, personal trainer or any other health professional, then find yourself a good one and start making small changes.

Improving your health, even just a little bit, will positively affect your decision-making abilities and overall attitude towards your work. The changes don't have to be massive, like suddenly running a marathon when you can barely jog to the end of the road. They can be small ones that build up over time and become easy-to-keep-up daily habits that just make you feel like a much better version of yourself. This in turn may lead to the realisation that you don't need to make a career change. You don't have to leave your job and start afresh. You just need to feel better about and within yourself, so that the small challenges you face on a daily basis remain 'small challenges' that are easily overcome and fade into insignificance when compared to all the benefits your existing role presents.

On the other hand, the new and improved, braver you may be able to look at your current work situation and see with unsullied clarity that it's time to move on. Either way, you'll be making a positive step in the right direction.

The power of sleep

You might be wondering why a book about changing jobs is addressing the power of sleep. The link may not be immediately obvious, so allow me to explain.

Lack of sleep can affect a whole host of things, which is why you'll hear some of the most productive and happy people in the world talking about how they now make sleep a priority in their lives. Among other things, sleep can affect:

- Your concentration levels.
- Your decision-making ability.
- Your weight.
- Your ability to deal with stressful situations.
- Your mood.
- Your immune system.
- Your hormones.

If you're on the cusp of making a life-changing decision, doesn't it make sense to be as rational and clear-headed about it as possible?

I love this simple, but highly effective good-night-sleep formula:

- 3 hours before bed – no food.
- 2 hours before bed – no drink.
- 1 hour before bed – no screen.

If you have a really good reason for not being able to get enough sleep at night, a daytime power nap may just become your new best friend.

The Japanese advocate the power of napping to such an extent that they have even named the practice of sleeping at work. They call it 'Inemuri'.

The Japanese power nap isn't limited to the workplace. A cafe in Tokyo offers upright sleeping pods for customers needing to catch a few winks. Inspired by the apparent fact that giraffes nap for 20 minutes each day standing up, the 'Giraffepod' is a phone booth-size pod, which allows its users to nap while standing up.

Nutrition

Despite the fact that there is no shortage of information about the effect of food and drink on our bodies and brains, many of us prefer to bury our heads in the sand about it. Again, you may be questioning why a book about career choices even mentions nutrition. I'm not a nutritionist, and this is not a book about nutrition. Yet it would be remiss of me not to highlight the correlation between what you consume and how you feel about your work.

Put simply, if you prioritise the consumption of healthy food and drink over the unhealthy alternatives you will likely:

- Feel better in and about yourself.
- Be able to cope with stressful situations more easily.
- Feel less tired and grumpy.
- Make overall better decisions.
- Have more energy.

As dramatic as it may sound, failing to make positive adjustments to your diet could lead to you walking away from a perfectly good job, only to realise afterwards that it wasn't the job but your general health that was making you feel dissatisfied.

Try this

Changes I can make immediately:

Sleep

Eg. make sure I get at least eight hours sleep per night.

Movement

Eg. go for a walk in nature for 30 minutes at least three days a week.

Nutrition

Eg. eat more fruit and veg, drink more water, drink less alcohol.

PART 7
Exploring what's possible

A change of scenery

Do you drive to work the same way every day? Do you spend most of your time with the same people? Do you read the same kind of books? Do you watch the same genre of TV programmes? Do you do the same thing every weekend? Do you follow the same kind of people or organisations on social media?

When's the last time you did something out of the ordinary?

It's easy to fall into the trap of living a life that feels like Groundhog Day. We find ourselves in the unrelenting cycle of daily chores and activities that "just have to be done". It's difficult to make good, life-changing decisions when we're in this state. Yet, when we consciously introduce a bit of novelty into our lives, things can start to look very different.

"A change of scenery is as good as a holiday."

I love this expression because I think it's so true! Even a little change can make a big difference.

If you're feeling *stuck* in a career that doesn't bring you much, or any, joy anymore, maybe you could do with a little change of scenery. Maybe all you need is a break from the norm.

If you have a holiday planned, that might just do the trick. But holidays, as lovely as they are, sometimes mean going to the same destination, with the same people, and doing familiar activities.

Make a plan to experience something completely different, in a different environment, with different people. This will help to create new neural pathways, which in turn will help you to think differently and very probably help you gain clarity. You might just find that it sparks a brand new interest, reminds you of a passion that you'd forgotten you had, and gives you a completely new and fresh perspective on life. That can't be a bad thing.

Meet Lucy

Having been made redundant from her job of 11 years at the National Trust, Lucy found herself at a bit of a loose end. She had little idea what she wanted to do next. She decided to put some of her redundancy money to good use and take her partner Colin on the trip of a lifetime: a road trip around the USA. While enjoying a glass of ale in a brewery in Wyoming, she announced to her partner that she'd like to try brewing her own beer. On the flight back to the UK, she could barely believe it when the inflight magazine (which she still has to this day!) featured an entire article about microbreweries in her home county. Seeing it as a sign, she started brewing beer in her garage as soon as she got back, and then selling at the local farmers' market not long after. Since then, she's created a thriving micro-brewery business... and is having the time of her life!

Taking time out

If you're a busy person with a hectic schedule, taking time out to reflect on your career might feel like an impractical, somewhat counter-intuitive, selfish and maybe even impossible thing to do. Our daily routines often don't allow much time for introspection or taking the time to be deliberate about the kind of lives we're creating for ourselves.

Many of us do feel like our calendar has to be jam-packed. We wear the phrase "I'm so busy" like a badge of honour. Somewhere along the line, we've convinced ourselves that being busy is something to aspire to. What's more, being busy and constantly on the go can feel fantastic. Many of us are addicted to the dopamine and adrenaline hit we get from being busy and in demand. The narrative we tell ourselves is that if we're busy, it means that we're in demand, and if we're in demand we're leading a meaningful life. However, if you're too busy to think, you're too busy to grow. It's as simple as that.

Ironically, just in the time it's taken me to write this chapter, I've had messages from four different friends saying:

"Just had a craaaaaazzzzzzy busy month. Sorry I haven't been in touch, just been flat out."

"All good, just seriously 100 mph. No rest for the wicked!"

"I haven't had a minute to myself."

"I've been burning the candle at both ends this week."

Unfortunately, being in this constant state of busyness can have a detrimental effect on our mental and physical health, and our relationships if we're not careful. I've definitely been there, done that, and got the t-shirt in every size and colour. I've been in jobs where, some days, taking a one-minute comfort break felt like pure luxury.

> *"Busy is the new stupid."*
>
> WARREN BUFFET

If you do a search for the phrase "busy is the new stupid" you will most likely encounter a video of Bill Gates talking about how Warren Buffet's calendar is almost empty and that we can all learn from that. You might argue that it's easy for two multi-billionaires to sit around talking about how we should all be more like Warren, because he's so rich that he and several subsequent generations in his family will never ever have to worry about earning a penny. His nonchalant remark, "I can buy anything I like, but I can't buy time", might even piss you off somewhat. You may feel that us mere mortals don't have the luxury of sitting around in deep contemplation.

I rarely encounter people who are deliberate about how they spend their time. But I will make the bold assertion that you do have some control over how you spend your precious time – whether you currently believe this to be true or not. How much of your busyness is your choice, and your choice alone?

As hard as it may seem to take time out from your busy schedule, the benefits of gifting yourself some time to take stock will ultimately be worth it.

There's something to be said for taking six months off to go travelling to 'find yourself'. It's an opportunity to gain new experiences and a fresh perspective on life. If you have the financial means and the support from loved ones to do so, then why not? Go for it!

The practicality of making an extended career break work is, for most people, simply not possible. Luckily, there are plenty of alternatives to taking a lengthy sabbatical.

Sometimes, it's simply a matter of being mindful about how you spend your time. Is what you spend your time on getting you closer to where you want to be, or keeping you in a place of despair or indecision? How can you carve out time for yourself to let your mind wander? Use your commute to listen to an audiobook that will inspire and delight you. Book yourself a room by the sea and watch the waves crash against the shore for a few hours. Go on a weekend retreat. In effect, you're already taking time out by reading this book, so that's something!

We all have 24 hours in a day, and when we say we don't have time for certain things that we'd like to have time for, what we really mean is that we're not prioritising said things.

We don't have time to think about our career, but we do have time to gossip with a friend.

We don't have time to think about our career, but we do have time to scroll through our Instagram feed. We don't have time to think about our career, but we do have time to listen to Radio 1 on our commute home.

That's not to say that you shouldn't spend time on any of these things. I just want to emphasise the fact that you probably do have time, you're possibly just choosing to spend it on things that are less important.

Activities that are fun and rewarding in the short-term give us a hit of dopamine, which is why we love spending time on them. But too often they rob us of precious time which could be invested in actually achieving the things we dream of.

Meet Georg

Georg felt like his career had plateaued and his values no longer aligned with those of his company, so he decided it was time to leave his job as Head of Innovation Accelerator for a Swiss insurance business. With the support of his wife, they decided to sell their family home in Holland, and moved themselves and their two young kids to Bali, an island in Indonesia they'd never been to before.

He was unsure of what he really wanted to do work-wise, so he embarked on what he refers to as "a year of creative endeavour". He started running ultra-marathons; learned music production; took a singing class; wrote, recorded and published his first song; tried freediving and spearfishing. By living off the money they'd made from the sale of their house, and using some of their savings, these endeavours enabled him to take time out to "unlearn all the things I'd picked up in corporate, and do things that I wanted to do – things that I enjoyed."

Georg is now enjoying his new life in Bali as a freelance Strategy and Innovation Coach and Consultant.

Skill up

Some career transitions are easily made, while some require a whole new set of skills and more experience. If you know you will need an additional qualification in your new role, why not embark on that evening or weekend course now, while you're still gainfully employed?

There are plenty of no- and low-cost adult education classes out there.

If you don't need an actual qualification, but would gain more confidence from a little more 'education' in a specific field, your options are endless. I often joke that you can probably learn as much from a carefully curated selection of YouTube videos as from a formal MBA. We're lucky to have information on absolutely any topic you can imagine at our fingertips nowadays.

Even if you never end up using your new skills and knowledge in your next job, you'll have spent quality time doing something that interests and energises you. You'll likely be a much more content, confident person as a result.

Be, Do, Have... Give

You may be familiar with the concept 'Be Do Have', which is often referred to in personal development and goal-setting.

In a nutshell, the premise is that one's identity and values (Be = ambitious, diligent, hard-working) guide our actions and behaviours (Do = get a good job, work hard) which in turn will lead to the attainment of goals and possessions (Have = the house, the marriage, the holidays, the cars, status, prestige).

It may well be that you have ticked each of the 'Be Do Have' boxes and now it's time to add a fourth element. What happens if we throw 'GIVE' into the mix? How would your attitude to work change if you reframed it from being a means of earning money, to your contribution to the world in a meaningful way?

If life has treated you well so far, and you have achieved all of your extrinsic goals, perhaps you'll find fulfillment by focusing on giving back – contributing to society in a more meaningful way.

It's one of life's least best-kept secrets that the best way to feel good about yourself is to do something good for someone else. It warms your heart and fosters an unrivalled sense of connection and belonging.

It's no coincidence that people who give back in a meaningful way, also report much higher levels of happiness. If you think this sounds far too airy fairy, wishy washy, new agey for you, here's a little bit of science.

The feeling of wellbeing and happiness we experience when we engage in altruistic acts can be attributed to the fact that our brain releases neuro chemicals like dopamine, oxytocin and endorphins. These are all associated with feelings of pleasure, reward, satisfaction, happiness and social bonding that far outweigh and outlast any pleasure we may derive from the purchase of a new handbag or yet another meal at a fancy restaurant.

It turns out that engaging with people, understanding their needs and emotions, and helping them in some way leads to a life with much more meaning and joy.

Meaning can be derived in different ways, and what feels meaningful will obviously vary from person to person. Just because someone finds meaning in ensuring big organisations play their part in sustainability, doesn't mean it will have the same effect for you. Working with young people to help them with their mental health issues might sound completely uninteresting to you, yet may be incredibly rewarding for someone else.

Here are some examples of how people 'give' through work:

- Working within an organisation that shares their values.
- Going into a teaching profession in order to inspire our next generation.
- Setting up an enterprise which focuses on solving social issues.
- Actively ensuring the business they run is genuinely focused on the wellbeing of their staff.
- Taking on a role which pays less than they're accustomed to, but enables them to share their experience and knowledge with people who really appreciate it.
- Taking on an advisory role.
- Offering to mentor younger people in or outside their organisation.

While many believe that the true definition of altruism is to be completely selfless and focused only on what will benefit others, you may have heard of 'selfish altruism'. Ultimately the concept of selfish altruism, also sometimes referred to as 'reciprocal altruism', is motivated by self-interest. Doing something good for others makes us feel good about ourselves. Studies have shown that even witnessing someone else engaging in a kind act makes us feel good.

It's a win-win situation.

In summary, it's selfless to be selfish.

Can you identify the 'Be Do Have pattern in your career? Is there room for 'Give' now?

Meet Sarah

Sarah had a successful career as a Sales Director in the giftware industry. Gradually she started to feel like she was falling out of love with her job, and eventually realised that she wasn't looking forward to her day each morning. She was feeling lacklustre about the sector, and a colleague reminding her that they were "selling tomorrow's landfill" just compounded that feeling.

It was while she was enjoying quality time with her family on holiday that she came to the realisation that life was short, and she wanted to do something that would have more meaning. She knew what she didn't want to do, but she didn't really have a clear idea of what she did want to do. She took the bold move of quitting her job before she really knew what she was going to do next.

After much soul-searching, and undeterred by the fact it was a completely new field for her, she eventually landed a job working for a charity that focuses on social mobility for young people.

"I'm really lucky that I work with an excellent group of people. I wake up every day with joy in my heart and look forward to the day ahead."

Starting a side hustle

Starting a side hustle in your spare time is an excellent way to test drive a business idea, while still having the security of regular income. Personally, I'm a big fan of a thrilling passion project in combination with the security of a job.

It's an exciting time to be going into business for yourself. The technology that we all have at our fingertips in this era, more than any other time in history, means, without exaggeration, that you can establish a brand new business in a single day – from your smartphone, from scratch, lying on your sofa, in your PJs (if you so wish), with little or even no financial investment. The barriers to starting a business have never been so low.

Apart from the potential to earn a bit (or a lot!) more money, there's a good chance a side hustle will ignite creativity, alleviate some of the tedium you may be feeling, enhance your skills, and generally lead to you enjoying your current job a lot more. It's a *positive* distraction.

This may be why corporations such as Google, Infusionsoft, Hubspot and Adobe actively encourage extra-curricular entrepreneurship.

I've spent a lot of time trying to work out why so many people who feel they'd like to change careers end up becoming self-employed. I think the reasons are multifaceted but, more often than not, boil down to the fact that people want more control over their working lives. They want more flexibility, more autonomy and they want their work to be as authentic to them as possible. They're done with making someone else richer, and they're done with trying to fall in line with someone else's vision, which they don't agree with, or can't get excited about.

If you have an idea for a business that excites you, what's stopping you from giving it a go?

Seek out all the free tools and resources available to you

There are literally millions of great books, podcasts and YouTube channels dedicated to start-ups. And most governments realise that small businesses are the backbone of their economy, and offer some kind of support to start-ups. All it takes to find them is a quick search online.

Create a business plan

As the well-known saying suggests "fail to plan, plan to fail". Apart from anything else, a business plan will help you feel more confident about your passion project. Contrary to popular belief, it doesn't have to be a super detailed 60,000-page plan that outlines every minute detail of your idea. Unless you're looking for funding! In which case you'll need a very detailed plan indeed, and may find it advantageous to recruit some professional help.

If, however, you're planning on bootstrapping your idea, you're fine to create a plan that details what the business idea is, who the main customers will be, your marketing strategy, set up costs etc. A quick online search will give you instant access to free business plan templates with varying degrees of complexity. Above anything else it should be a document that keeps you focused, inspired and motivated.

Surround yourself with people who have done it

If you end up turning your seedling of an idea into a fully-fledged business, you'll most likely find that becoming your own boss is an emotional roller-coaster ride. Be under no illusion that the journey won't challenge you in ways you never dreamed of, and that you'll learn so much about yourself and others. If you can surround yourself with people who have entrepreneurial experience, it will make things much more fun and easier to navigate.

Meet Ben

Ben knew from a very young age that he wanted to be a Dyson engineer. He fulfilled his dream and absolutely loved his role as Principal Engineer. However, early on in his career, he was asked to help out with small side projects outside of his nine-to-five. This led to the realisation for him that he could have more than one income stream. Amongst many other things, outside of his main job he also created full branding and printed literature for several companies, designed the safety system for the world's tallest salmon ladder and launched a kids innovation club.

"I have a natural need to be creative. And I love making and creating; I've been doing it my entire life. It turns out that people seem to really like the things I make – and seem to want to give me money for them."

After years of being a 'Toe-Dipper', Ben found that his side hustles were taking up more and more of his time. What's more, he felt he was destined for more. He finally made the leap and quit his dream job at Dyson in October 2023.

"It got to the point where Dyson was more like a hobby than the day job… There was this opportunity to own my own time, own my own income with

pretty much no ceiling on what that could possibly be. And it was an opportunity too great to say no to. And at that point, you're like, okay, I can't do everything... I've put myself in hospital this year, so I can't continue to do everything. And this opportunity here is just screaming at me. I can't keep telling kids about mindset and about positive attitude and achieving dreams and that kind of stuff, and then don't do it myself. So I was like, right, we're doing this. We're gonna make this happen".

Volunteering

Volunteering your time when it already feels like there aren't enough hours in the day, can seem like a hugely counterproductive thing to do.

However, there are many reasons why volunteering in a field that interests you – even for a couple of hours a month – can have huge benefits for you:

- You never know who you might meet or what you might be inspired by.
- You'll most likely develop new skills.
- You'll gain new experiences and thus adopt a fresh perspective on life.
- It allows you to test the waters in a new career or industry without making a major commitment.
- It can help build confidence.
- It will enhance your CV.
- It might lead to a paid job within the organisation.

The list of positives is endless and a benefit that warrants special mention is that volunteering can have such a dramatic effect on us that it inspires us to take our careers in a whole new direction.

Find a stopgap

Depending on who you speak to, you'll receive favourable and much less favourable attitudes towards stopgaps. Personally, I don't think there's anything wrong with a stopgap. In fact, there are many reasons why a stopgap can be just what you need.

Stopgaps are great if:

- You desperately want to get out of your current role.
- You're not completely sure what you want to do.
- You want/need to earn money while you're working out what your next career move is going to be.
- You enjoy meeting new people.

A stopgap job can also be really helpful in working out what you *don't* enjoy doing.

The idea of a stopgap, as the name suggests, is that you won't do it forever. But then sometimes you hit the jackpot with your 'temporary' job, and stumble across something you absolutely love. What's more, you never know what other opportunities the stopgap may lead to.

Working part-time

What would happen if you suddenly had an extra day or two to yourself every week? How would you spend that time? Would it allow you to have more time with family and friends? Would you be able to exercise more? Could you start a side hustle?

If you think that asking your employer to work part-time instead of full-time is 'career suicide' then there is a chance you may be right. There are still people, and hence organisations, that take the stance that you have to work full-time (and ideally more!) if you are to be taken seriously. They still hold the belief that part-time workers are less valuable to the organisation.

The managing director of a large distribution company confided in me: "I just feel like our part-time staff are less invested in the success of our business. Like they are prioritising everything else above the work they are expected to do here."

Bear with me here, because it's not all bad news. On the contrary! The great news is that there has been a massive mind shift with respect to part-time work over the last few years. Progressive organisations that truly value and care for their people recognise that part-time staff are just as valuable as their full-time counterparts. They may work fewer hours, but are often totally focused and driven within those hours. They don't spend three hours a day chatting by the water cooler, wasting precious time with idle gossip. They appreciate the fact that their organisation allows them flexibility, and consequently reciprocate with hard work, dedication and loyalty.

If going part-time is an option for you financially, and you have some great ideas of what you could do with the extra time, it may well be worth exploring.

Here are some tips to make part-time work for you:

- Network with the right people who will help you build your profile even when you're not in the office.
- Identify a sponsor within senior management who supports you and will cheerlead for you when you're not in the room.
- Put yourself forward for working groups that interest you.
- Prove that you can be just as effective, if not more so, within your new reduced hours.
- Raise your personal profile externally too by using platforms such as LinkedIn.
- Become an excellent relationship-builder, and become an indispensable linchpin.
- If you job-share, ensure you have a super-close and supportive working relationship with the person you're job-sharing with. Have very specific handovers and leave nothing open to interpretation.
- Be very clear with yourself and others about your specific work objectives.
- Set boundaries so people know when you are available and when you're not. Ensure that you aren't being paid a part-time salary for full-time hours.
- Be prepared for the fact that some full-time colleagues *may* resent you. They may feel you're less committed, and there's a good chance that they'll be a little bit envious of your newfound freedom.

It's generally easier to reduce your existing hours with your current employer than to start looking for part-time work elsewhere, but if your current employer is totally closed off to the idea of reducing your hours, then looking elsewhere might be a viable option.

Meet Natalie

If you'd met Natalie a few years ago and asked her what she did for a living, she would have lit up and gladly shared with you the intricate details of her work and how meaningful it was to her.

In 2023, things started to change. Actually, she changed. Her outlook on life and her priorities shifted. She became disillusioned with the organisation she was working for, and started seeking more fulfilment.

At one point it got so bad that she planned to quit her job completely. However, she wasn't quite sure what she wanted to do instead, so didn't feel ready to jump into another role immediately. Being the main breadwinner, she had her reservations about putting her family under financial pressure. Crucially, her closest family members – her husband and mother – were supportive and fully behind her, whatever she decided. After a lot of soul-searching, she decided that going part-time might be a viable option, and give her the time and headspace she needed to explore her options a bit more.

She did her research and familiarised herself with the organisation's policy around part-time work. Then she put together a strong case for why she wanted to drop her hours from five days to three days per week, and presented it to her line manager. Together they worked on a plan for handing over some of the projects that Natalie had been working on and really focused her time on just a few key areas.

Now Natalie works her reduced hours, she feels incredibly liberated at having let go of projects that weren't part of her core job, and that she didn't find particularly exciting in the first place. "I'm so much more efficient and focused now that I'm juggling fewer things at work. My priorities are much clearer and I'm getting more done".

The extra time has enabled a healthier work-life balance that better suits her current circumstances. She's using the additional hours to spend more time with her daughter, and prioritise health and wellbeing, and caring for her mother. It's also giving her time to explore her main passion, which is regenerative farming.

Seek out a secondment

A secondment is often a safe way to get unstuck if you're in a role that doesn't feel right. In case you're not familiar with what a secondment is, it's basically a temporary work placement in a different department or even another company. It's usually for a fixed and predetermined amount of time. You're likely to earn the same or, in some instances, even more than your current salary, so there's very little risk involved.

It's an experience which is likely to give you deeper insight into what you do and don't enjoy. There's a good chance it will give you a newfound appreciation of the day-to-day activities, familiar environment and perhaps even of your colleagues in your current role.

It could however also do the exact opposite and expose you to a whole new exciting world. New projects, new colleagues, a new environment, unfamiliar assignments, and the opportunity to embark on a new learning experience.

Research

What knowledge would make you feel more in control of your career path? What insight would give you an advantage? Do your research.

- Talk to people who have experience in the field you'd like to enter.
- Connect with people who work for the organisation you are interested in joining.
- Look into what new qualifications you may need to acquire.
- Find out all you can about the organisation you would love to work for.
- What are some growing trends in your industry?
- What is your earning potential?

PART 8
Your people

The people in our lives can be our greatest motivators – or our greatest obstacles. They either get us closer to the life we want, or further away from it. Most people around us fall into one of those two categories. Very few fall into neither.

Your support network

Isolation may have crept up on us during Covid, but it's still having a dramatic impact on our lives! Many of us are spending more time alone, staring at a screen for most of the day. We're missing out on human interaction which, even for introverts, is crucial. We're inherently social creatures, and having that human connection is paramount for our physical health, and our mental and emotional wellbeing. Even Microsoft's CEO Satya Nadella acknowledges that "digital technology should not be a substitute for human connection".

However, merely spending quality time with other people may not be enough. You'll remember from the chapter on 'Beliefs' that so many of the beliefs we carry are 'caught', and not 'taught'. So it stands to reason that the people we spend most of our time with have a huge impact on how we think, act and what we believe is possible. Whether or not you buy into the saying "you are the average of the five people you spend the most time with", there's no getting away from the fact that the people in our network can serve us – or hold us back.

The people you choose to spend the most time with over coming weeks, months and years are very likely to have a huge impact on your career. They will have a massive impact on how likely you are to achieve what you set out to do. You can make a change to your career without the right crowd around you, but it's going to be a much smoother ride *with* the right people. It's so much easier doing things that we perceive as 'hard' when we feel supported by people we admire, whose opinion we trust, and who are interested in, and excited about, us succeeding.

Cheerleaders

Sometimes all it takes is for someone to believe in us and our abilities in order for us to move metaphorical mountains. One of the common threads I observe when talking to people who have made fruitful career changes, is that they have a life partner who is supportive of their dreams and aspirations. Partners make great cheerleaders, because they generally know you very well, love you, want the best for you and know that your happiness will also have a knock-on effect on them.

But your best cheerleaders don't always come in the form of a wife, husband, boyfriend or girlfriend.

A cheerleader can be anyone in your tribe who totally gets what you're aiming for and thinks you're the bee's knees for doing so. They want to support you in any way they can and are committed to your growth. They believe in you, even at times when you don't. These people are good for our soul and, let's be honest, our self-confidence. They lift us when we're having a bad day. Remind us of just how far we've come. Encourage us to follow our dreams. They just make the whole journey so much more fun and worthwhile.

Who are your cheerleaders in life? Your first instinct may be that you don't have any currently. As luck would have it, the world is full of people who want the best for others. Now all you have to do is tune in to finding them. And they'll come out of the woodwork for you.

Coach

Over the years coaches have, unfortunately, received some negative press. Feel free to accuse me of being biased, but I have way too much personal evidence to know that a good coach is worth their weight in gold.

Let's go back to basics and look at what a good coach is. A good coach will ask you all the right questions, and listen to you without judgement. It's someone who gently challenges you without a hidden agenda or personal bias. Someone who'll help you uncover, and encourage you to listen to, the absolute best version of yourself. They'll likely see things in you that you can't. They will help to quieten your inner critic and dial up the voice that is compassionate and cheering you on to fulfil your potential.

Your coach should be someone who has coaching qualifications, is highly skilled at asking all the right questions and listens without judgement. Ideally, they'd come highly recommended by people who have first-hand experience of their professionalism. Want an easy way to spot a coach who may be less proficient? If they love talking about themselves and spend way more time telling you about how fabulous they are than paying genuine interest in you, I would say that's a very loud and clear warning sign.

Role models

A role model can be someone you know, but it can also be someone you know of. In order to find your role models, ask yourself who is already leading the life you'd love to be living. Who do you look up to? Who do you know who's thriving in their career, and grins ear to ear when they talk about their work? Find out why their work is making them so happy.

You don't have to love absolutely everything about them, their life and career. You can pick and choose aspects of their way of earning a living that appeals to you and that you may be able to emulate. You can follow them on social media, read their books, listen to interviews they've given, or even ask to connect with them.

Try this

- Write a list of people you already know who can help you get to where you want to be.
- Who are the people you don't already know who you would like to have within your support network?
- Who do you know who has already done what you'd like to do?

Dealing with people who don't want you to make a change

Are the people who are closest to you fully supportive of your desire to quit your job and do something new? Do you have only people in your life who totally get you and your dreams, and are 100 per cent behind you? Do they cheer you on and encourage you no matter what? If so, you have my full permission to feel a little bit smug and bask in that rather fortuitous situation. You can also skip this chapter if you choose.

What do you do if you're totally fired up to take control and make changes to your career that you know for sure are going to make you happier, and people try to stop you from making those changes? This could be your husband, wife, live-in lover, best friend, parent, sibling. If you have someone, or indeed more than one person in your life, who is not supportive of you making a career change, this chapter is for you.

First of all, you're not alone! In all my research, not having the support from the people we care for most, is one of the biggest obstacles to initiating change. Facing a situation where you are not supported by people who are important to you can be incredibly emotionally challenging, so I hope this section makes it a little bit easier for you.

Chief Dream Squisher

The Chief Dream Squisher (CDS) is someone who will sometimes intentionally, but also often completely unintentionally, squish your dreams. They are the people who will go out of their way to discourage you from making any changes to your life.

Our nearest and dearest can sometimes unwittingly be our biggest opponents.

Because these people are dear to us, we take their objections very personally, and very seriously. We don't want to upset them, and we certainly don't want to disappoint them. Sometimes, these are the people we love and respect most, so it's hard to understand why they would want to squish our dreams.

Their reasons for doing this will vary:

They're fearful about how the change will affect *them*
We've already explored how our fears and beliefs can be our biggest blockers for change. Just because you've overcome your fears, it doesn't mean other people will follow suit.

They are content with how things are, and *your* career change may not fit in with *their* goals and aspirations for you.

They're worried about how the change will affect *you*
A CDS can be someone who genuinely cares deeply for you and wants the best for you, but holds an ardent belief that making a change is going to have a negative effect on you. They want to keep you safe. However, in most instances they are merely projecting their fears onto you.

They're worried that you're making a big mistake and want to protect you from that. They may be concerned that you're throwing your career away, that you'll earn a lot less money or you'll be unhappier in your next role. Perhaps they genuinely believe that your life is fine just the way it is, and change is completely unnecessary. They're fervent supporters of 'better the devil you know'.

It suits them for you to stay exactly where you are right now. Where you are now is predictable and safe, as far as they're concerned. You're safe, they're safe.

If they can't make you 'see sense', they may resort to sneaky emotional manipulation to make you feel guilty for being selfish. They may tell you they support you, all the while reminding you about the undesirable consequences of your plans.

They're scared of you succeeding

If you succeed in doing what you love, where does that leave them? Will they be jealous that you have found something that you are excited about, while they are stuck doing something they don't enjoy? Will it be a stark and constant reminder that they wasted their life in a job they hated?

If someone says they're worried about you throwing away all that time and money spent on your education and career to date, what are they actually opposing?

How to communicate effectively with your CDS

1. Have you already had the conversation with your CDS? Have you actually spoken to them, or are you making assumptions about how they might react? It's not uncommon to dream up a conversation with a CDS that doesn't go the way we'd like, and then never actually have the conversation because we're scared of the outcome we've imagined. We decide it's best to leave that particular stone unturned, and close the door on our dreams before we've given them half a chance. More often than not our brain predicts the worst case, as this is its way of preparing us for the fight. So we go into the conversation with a battle mentality, ready for a fight.

2. What if you went into the conversation expecting the best? You may not get the outcome you desire right away, but you'll almost certainly enter the conversation in a much more amiable state. This will allow you to bring your carefully thought-through case across in a coherent, non-threatening manner, and is less likely to get your CDS's back up from the get-go.

3. Determine just how important the CDS's opinion really is to you. Who are you listening to? Will any changes you make *actually* affect them? How important is the opinion of someone who has never done anything worth celebrating in their life, who is absolutely *not* going to be affected by your actions?

4. Write a list of people who your actions are likely to impact directly, and whose opinion does matter to you. Next to their names write a couple of sentences about how your career change is likely to affect them.

5. Remember that this is a negotiation. You have to find some common ground so you can both feel okay with the final decision. There may be some compromises to be made on both sides. Where are you willing to compromise? Where are you absolutely not willing to compromise?

6. Prepare a well thought-through plan of how you're going to make the transition. How long will it take? How much is it likely to cost? What will be the outcome? What is your life likely to look like in a year; in three years; in 10 years? What's the 'worst case scenario'? What's your Plan B? Include any questions you think they might want answers to.

7. Carve out time when you're both relaxed, and won't be distracted. Present your plan to them. Be concise and explain why this is so important to you. Don't be afraid to show your passion and excitement. Remember, passion and excitement is (generally) contagious, and you can't expect them to be enthusiastic about your transition unless you are. Make your vision as vivid as possible for them. Share that you have a clear plan, and that you have spent a lot of time thinking about it. You're not just doing it on a whim. Share why this is so important to you.

8. Gauge their reaction and answer any questions they may have. Listen carefully to their perspective and find out exactly what their objections are without interrupting. Even though you might not want to hear them, do encourage them to voice their reservations and concerns about how your plans might impact your finances, your relationship or other important aspects of your lives.

9. Let them know that you have already considered these things, and if they raise concerns you haven't previously considered, let them know that you take their concerns seriously.

10. Tell them you appreciate their opinion and try not to get emotional if they're not on board straight away. They will need time to process and take a little while to get their head around your plan. Very few people accept big changes easily. So even if their initial reaction isn't to grab their pom poms and do a happy dance, that doesn't mean they won't eventually be supportive once they have had time to digest what you've presented to them. Take time to explore their fears and insecurities together. Show compassion for their fears.

11. Be open to the possibility that our CDS is presenting a logical reason as to why your career transition might not be viable, or the timing might not be ideal. Sometimes you have to agree to disagree. If this is the case for you, then it's about finding a compromise. What are possible scenarios that both parties could make peace with? For example, could you reduce the hours you currently work, and spend more time on activities that are important to you? Making positive progress in your desired new career may just be enough to convince your CDS that you are actually on the right track.

12. Evaluate the consequences of going against their wishes. How will this affect your relationship? Sometimes following our dreams does mean that we have to make difficult decisions and act in a way that will upset people, at least in the short-term. What are the

consequences of you not following your dreams? What is going to hurt you and others more in the long-term?

A useful template for having the conversation with your CDS:

- Why I feel discontent in my current situation.
- What I'd like to be doing instead.
- Why this is so important to me.
- How I'm going to achieve this.
- I acknowledge this will have an impact on the following...
- My way to mitigate this is...
- The research I've undertaken.
- What would need to happen for them to agree to your proposed change?
- Where can a compromise be reached?

Of course you always have the option of not running your plans by those who matter, and only telling them afterwards. While I'm not a fan of making sweeping generalisations, my research revealed that on the whole, men were less likely to be concerned about the opinions of others or the consequences of their actions. One man I spoke to was very open about the fact that he didn't consult his wife before quitting his 25-year career in the military. He didn't even have a plan beyond telling his boss he'd had enough. He took the bold stance that he would just "figure it out". The fact that he now runs a multi-million pound business doesn't change the fact that his wife is still unhappy with him about the decision he made almost 20 years ago.

Women tend to take a more collaborative approach, being more considerate about how their actions might impact those around them, in many cases giving up on their dreams altogether when they come across the first negative reaction from someone.

Ultimately, it's worth remembering that no matter which direction you decide to take your career in, the people who genuinely care about you, will want to see you happy.

PART 9
Conclusion

What's it going to be?

"Life is a matter of choices, and every choice you make makes you."

JOHN C. MAXWELL

I hope you've enjoyed the journey of self-discovery this book has taken you on. You may remember that in the very first chapter I talked about the four possible outcomes of reading this book. Are you a Remainer, Tweaker, Toe-dipper or Leaper™? Here's a recap.

Remainer: Your job is not the true source of your discontentment. Alternatively, you've come to the realisation that all jobs go through peaks and troughs, and you now feel reassured in the knowledge that you were just experiencing a slump in your current role. You've decided not to make any major changes to your existing career or job, but are approaching your work with renewed energy. You have a much more positive attitude towards it, and as a result enjoy it a whole lot more. You feel like you've regained control of your destiny.

Tweaker: You've come to the conclusion that you actually enjoy your current work and everything that comes with it. All you need is to make some adjustments. A few tweaks here and there will make all the difference to your satisfaction levels.

Toe-dipper: You're not quite ready to quit your job, but are keen to embark on an endeavour that sits outside of your current role. You'll spend your spare time in pursuit of a fun activity that is also likely to earn you some extra money.

Leaper: You're going for it! You've done your research. You've had all the right conversations. You've got a plan. You're ready to quit your job in search of a new adventure! Exciting, challenging and rewarding times ahead.

If I had a penny for every time someone told me they were worried about making the wrong decision, I'd be a multi-millionaire. Ultimately, there is no such thing as a 'bad' or 'wrong' decision. It's just a decision. Your perception and attitude towards every choice you make, coupled with the actions you take subsequently, will make them feel good or bad to you.

The other thing to remember is that whatever you decide to do today doesn't mean you can't change your mind later down the line. As we all know, things change. You may be a 'Remainer' today and a 'Leaper' tomorrow. Even if it feels like you've made the 'wrong' decision, that doesn't mean you can't change course down the line. You can never be the victim of a decision you've made, unless you allow yourself to be.

> *"Everything will be okay in the end. If it's not okay, it's not the end."*
>
> JOHN LENNON

Handing in your resignation

If you have indeed decided that you are going to be a 'Leaper' and are ready to quit your job, writing your resignation letter may be the most satisfying thing you ever write. It may also be the most terrifying. Perhaps even a combination of the two.

Ideally you want to leave the door open by leaving on the best terms possible. If the organisation you're leaving has treated you well, make sure you express your gratitude when you hand in your resignation. It's not a bad idea to publicly thank your employers for the opportunities they've given you. Thank your boss, your colleagues and anyone else who has helped you in your career to date. Few people don't like to be shown appreciation.

The U-turn

You may well find that your employer has a sudden appreciation for you as soon as your resignation letter hits their desk. At the time of writing, there is a huge skills shortage in the UK in certain areas, which means that companies will do their best to retain good staff. If your employer is adamant they would like you to stay, how will this affect your decision to leave? If they incentivise you to stay, is there an amount of money, a particular role, a side project they could offer you that would make you reconsider your decision? If there is, I would strongly recommend thinking about what those could be first. And then it may work to your advantage to talk to your boss about whether there are opportunities within your organisation that would make you stay. Present those ideas, see what happens. If there is no room for manoeuvre, then it's definitely time to embark on your new adventure.

Short-term pain, long-term gain

"Difficult roads often lead to beautiful destinations."

ZIG ZIGLAR

Now that you have a much clearer vision of what you want, coupled with the determination to achieve it, there's little that will stand in your way. In all likelihood, any change you make is initially going to feel uncomfortable. Saying goodbye to colleagues, leaving behind what you know, stepping out of that comfort zone. They'll all demand a positive attitude, unwavering self-belief and courage. Remind yourself that the hardship you're likely to encounter in the short-term is worth the reward that's ultimately on offer.

Patience and faith

Patience and faith are two things that we seem to lack in this day of instant gratification. In a world where we can access information on pretty much anything we want within two seconds, we have increasingly grown to expect everything to happen quickly, almost as soon as we've had the thought.

Don't get frustrated if you don't end up doing work you love immediately. It might take days, weeks, months or even years of exploring and experimenting. The key is to approach it like you would approach any adventure that promises to be exciting. Appreciate that your career path is a journey, not a destination. It can be really fun if you make it so, and the more fun you decide to make it, the more likely you are to enjoy it. Perceiving it as a burden and something that must be resolved as quickly as possible will, in most likelihood, put pressure on you and make it a stressful, unpleasant experience. If you can make peace with this fact, have a strong vision, backed by the faith that everything will work out just fine, perhaps you can learn to enjoy the feeling of unease.

When the faith in your vision is greater than your fear, then you can stop the fear controlling you. Whenever you experience a setback and can keep the faith that you're on the right track, it will give you the impetus and strength to continue.

Plan B

There are different opinions on whether it's a good idea to have a Plan B in life. Personally, I like having a Plan B; something I can fall back on if things don't go the way I hope and expect them to. While I'm yet to resort to a Plan B, I relish having a safety net because I don't love putting myself under a huge amount of unnecessary pressure. Others love being under pressure, and indeed find that's the only way for them to stay focused on the end result. Find and do what works best for you.

One final thing

Our work is much more than a means of earning a living. It's often the seedbed of our social life. It's an integral part of our identity. A way to express ourselves. A way to contribute to society. As cheesy as it may sound to you, it's a means of feeding our souls.

I'm all for a good plan that you feel happy with, but there comes a time when you just have to take action. Too often I come across people who complain about their job situation, and genuinely seem to want to make a change. However, their actions are not at all aligned with their desired outcome. They want to be offered a better job, but aren't willing to spend a bit of time creating a CV that will blow their competition out of the water. They want to be in a job that's aligned with their values, but aren't willing to go out of their way to meet with people who are well-positioned to give them a leg up.

If you are ardently dedicated to making a change, you are going to have to take action. The results you desire will follow your action only with positive and focused intention. Make action a habit. Nothing amazing will happen by simply daydreaming about it. If you're miserable in your job, as a bare minimum, take some action to feel less unhappy. Don't be one of those people who reads a book or attends a workshop, gets all fired up to make a positive change, and then does nothing. You owe it to yourself, those who love you, and the wider community. Your happiness, or lack thereof, has an enigmatic ripple effect on everyone and everything around you, whether you realise it or not. So if anyone ever accuses you of being selfish for following your dreams, do feel free to remind them that you're doing it for the greater good!

The most difficult part of any new endeavour is taking the first step. Whatever you've decided to do, go for it and have fun. You got this!

> *"The act of taking the first step is what separates the winners from the losers."*
>
> BRIAN TRACY

Thank yous

Thank you to my husband, who has been endlessly patient with me while I've written this book. Thank you for believing in me and for being my rock!

Thank you to my gorgeous daughters who inspire and make me laugh every day. Thank you for your faith in me, and for automatically assuming that this book would sell by the millions.

Thank you to my parents for instilling a 'can do' attitude in me and for being my biggest cheerleaders.

Thank you to my amazing, talented cousin, friend and editor Caroline. You are an absolute gem and I'm so lucky to have you in my life.

Thank you to my dear friend Susanne, who believed in me when others didn't, challenged and encouraged me the whole way. This book wouldn't have happened without your friendship and support, and I'll be eternally grateful to you.

Thank you to all my podcast guests, who have been so generous with their time and their willingness to share their stories and wisdom.

Thank you to my clients, who allowed me to share snippets of their stories to inspire others.

Thank you to Gail for being my sounding board for so many things. I really appreciate your wisdom.

Thank you to Joe for his invaluable advice to let my ideas "marinade" and not rush this book.

Thank you to all my family and friends who have put up with me starting every other sentence with "in my book..." for the last 18 months. I'll stop talking about it now. Or maybe I won't!

Appendix

www.yescareercoaching.com

Your Big Career Move podcast – available on Apple, Spotify and YouTube

Connect with me on LinkedIn – https://www.linkedin.com/in/yesimnicholson

Links to businesses mentioned in the book

Hannah: facebook.com/hghsportsmassage
Jen: wildfirewalks.com
Laura: glowinnovation.com
Michael: goldensheepcoffee.co.uk
Sarah: pyramidcc.co.uk
Anthony: flowsforlife.com
David: davidkingstonecarving.com
Shane: limor.ie
Danny: shortstoryventures.com
Koj: chefkoj.com
Nigel: nigelmarsh.com
Martin: knightsbeekeeping.co.uk
Natasa & Jim: wellnesstory.world
Lucy: coriniumales.co.uk

Printed in Great Britain
- by Amazon